The Le
Campaig

The Leipzig Campaign: 1813

Napoleon and the "Battle of the Nations"

F. N. Maude

LEONAUR

The Leipzig Campaign: 1813—Napoleon and the "Battle of the Nations"
by F. N. Maude

Published by Leonaur Ltd

ISBN: 978-1-84677-249-8 (hardcover)
ISBN: 978-1-84677-250-4 (softcover)

http://www.leonaur.com

Contents

Maps

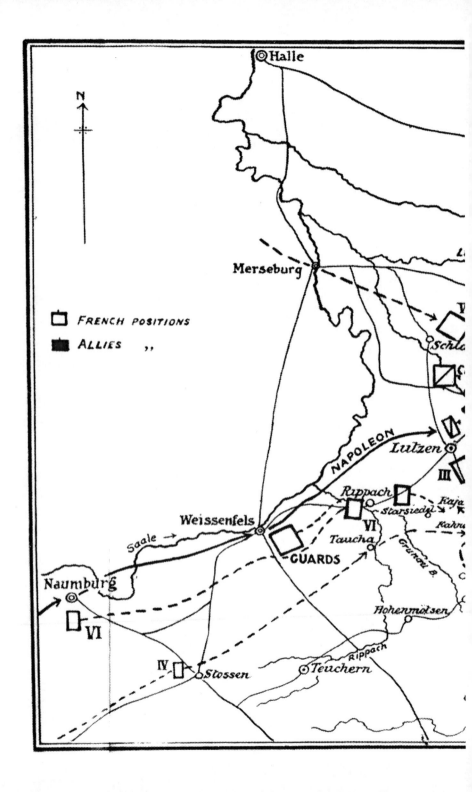

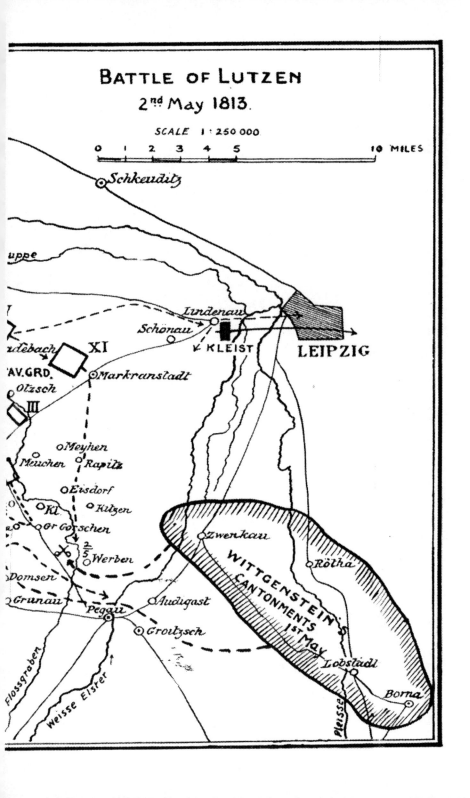

BATTLE OF LUTZEN
2nd May 1813.

SCALE 1 : 250 000

0 1 2 3 4 5   10 MILES

Schkeuditz

uppe

Lindenau

Schönau

V. KLEIST

LEIPZIG

debach   XI

AV. GRD.

Markranstadt

Otzsch

III

Meyhen

Meuchen   Rapitz

Eisdorf

Kl   Kitzen

Gr Gorschen

2/5 Werben

Domsen

Grunau   Pegau

Audigast

Groitzsch

Zwenkau

Rötha

WITTGENSTEIN'S
CANTONMENTS
1st May

Lobstädt

Borna

Flossgraben

Weisse Elster

Pleisse

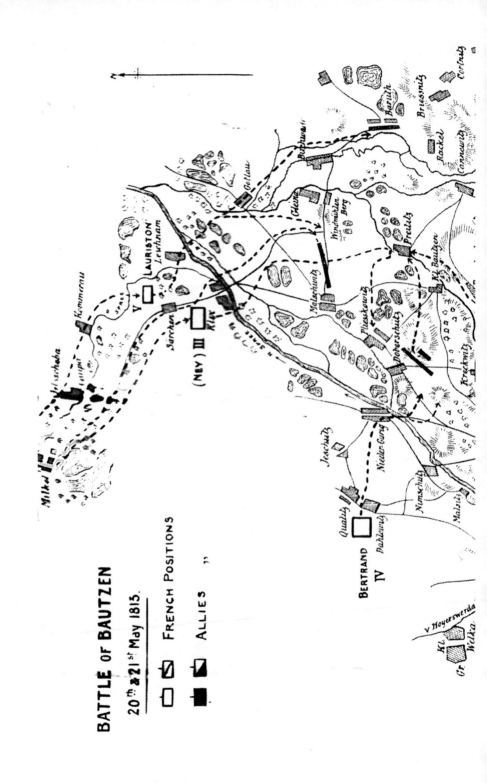

BATTLE of BAUTZEN

20th & 21st May 1815.

◫ FRENCH POSITIONS
◩ "
▢ ALLIES "
◼

N

LAURISTON Leuthum

V

(NEY) III

Klix

BERTRAND IV

Dahlowitz

Quatitz

Jeschütz

Niedersung

Nimschütz

Malsitz

v Hoyerswerda

Kl. Welka

Gr. Welka

Kreckwitz

Doberschütz

Plusskowitz

N. Bautzen

Preititz

Malschwitz

Windmühlen Berg

Gleina

Gottlau

Burghwass

Baruth

Briessnitz

Racket

Canneswitz

Corbitz

Sarchen

Kommerau

Nochoba

Milkel

V

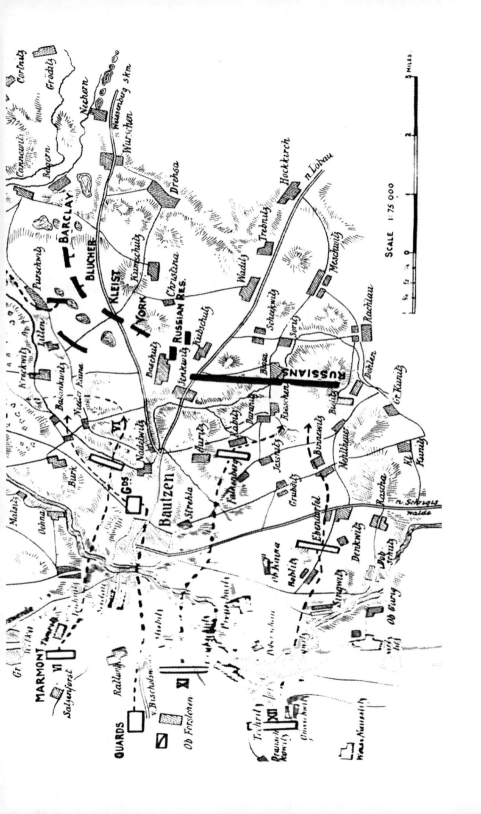

Scale 1:75000

| 1 | 3/4 | 1/2 | 1/4 | 0 | | 1 | | 2 | | 3 MILES |

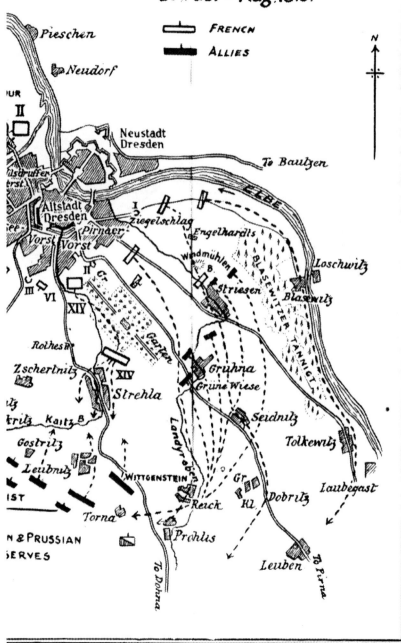

BATTLE OF DRESDEN

26ᵗʰ & 27ᵗʰ Aug. 1813.

FRENCH

ALLIES

N

Pieschen

Neudorf

Neustadt
Dresden

To Bautzen

ELBE

Altstadt
Dresden

Ziegelschlag

Engelhardts

Windmühlen

Pirnaer
Vorst.

B.

Striesen

Loschwitz

Blasewitz

BLASEWITZER TÄNNIGT

Rothes

Garten

Gruhna

Grune Wiese

Zschertnitz

Strehla

Seidnitz

Tolkewitz

Kaitz

Gostritz

Leubnitz

WITTGENSTEIN

Gr.

Kl.

Dobritz

Laubegast

N & PRUSSIAN
RESERVES

Torna

Reick

Prohlis

To Dohna

Leuben

To Pirna

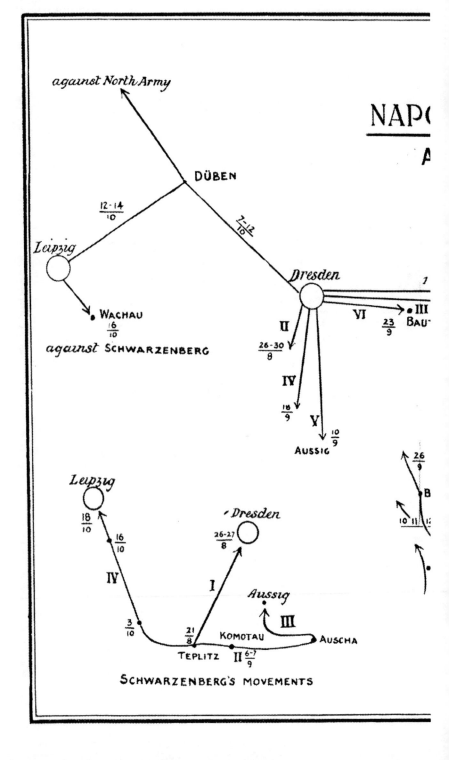

against North Army

DÜBEN

$\frac{12-14}{10}$

$\frac{7-12}{10}$

Leipzig

Dresden

Wachau
$\frac{16}{10}$

against Schwarzenberg

II
$\frac{26-30}{8}$

VI $\frac{23}{9}$

III
Bau...

IV
$\frac{18}{9}$

V
$\frac{10}{9}$

Aussig

NAPO...

A...

1

$\frac{26}{9}$

B

10 11 1...

Leipzig
$\frac{18}{10}$

$\frac{16}{10}$

IV

$\frac{3}{10}$

Dresden
$\frac{26-27}{8}$

I

$\frac{21}{8}$

Teplitz

Komotau

II $\frac{6-7}{9}$

Aussig

III

Auscha

SCHWARZENBERG'S MOVEMENTS

DIAGRAM OF ...OLEON'S MOVEMENTS

AUGUST—OCTOBER 1813.

Scale $\dfrac{1}{1\,000\,000}$

1st Offensive

LOWENBERG
$\dfrac{21\text{-}22}{8}$

GOLDBERG
$\dfrac{23}{8}$

II
UTZEN

GORLITZ
$\dfrac{4\text{-}5}{9}$

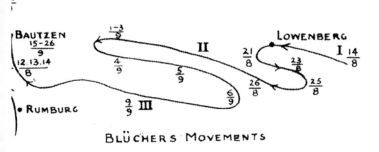

BAUTZEN
$\dfrac{15\text{-}26}{9}$

$\dfrac{12.13.14}{8}$

$\dfrac{1\text{-}3}{9}$

$\dfrac{4}{9}$

$\dfrac{5}{9}$

$\dfrac{6}{9}$

II

LOWENBERG

$\dfrac{21}{8}$

$\dfrac{23}{8}$

$\dfrac{26}{8}$

$\dfrac{25}{8}$

I $\dfrac{14}{8}$

RUMBURG

$\dfrac{9}{9}$ III

BLÜCHER S MOVEMENTS

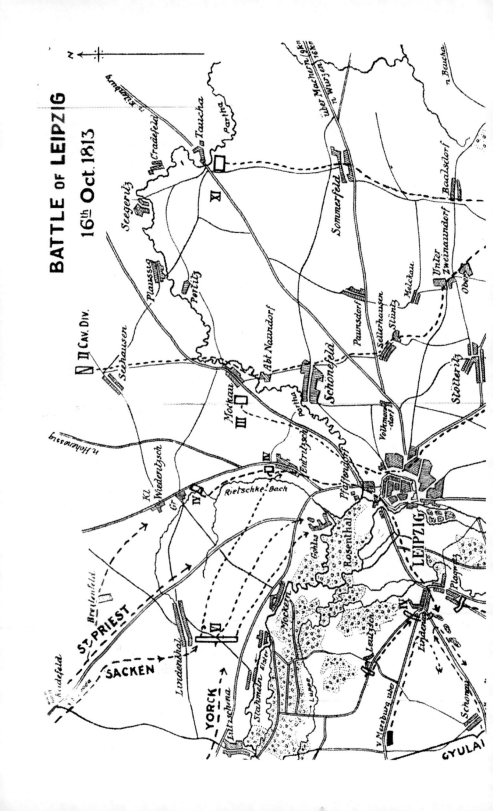

BATTLE of LEIPZIG
16th Oct. 1813

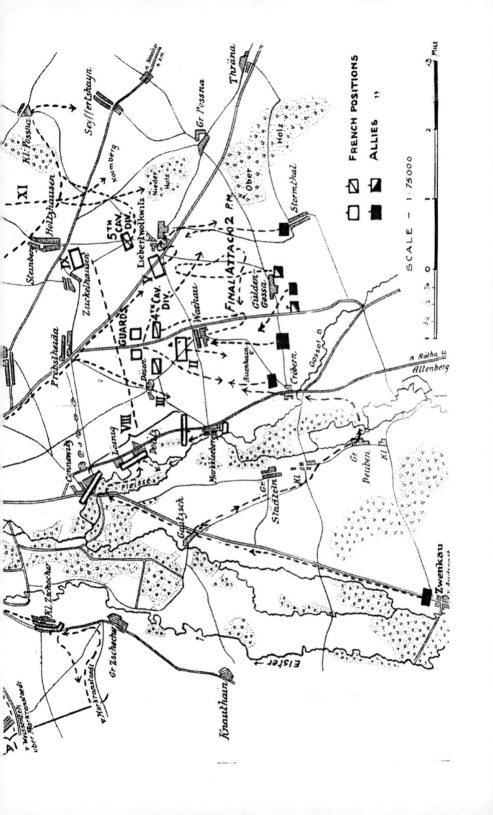

FRENCH POSITIONS
ALLIES ⁾

SCALE — 1:75000

Introduction

"Alors, un homme s'élèvera, peut-être resté jusque-là dans la foule et l'obscurité, un homme qui ne se sera fait un nom ni par ses paroles, ni par ses écrits un homme qui aura médité dans le silence, un homme enfin qui aura peut-être ignoré son talent, qui ne l'aura senti qu'en l'exerçant, et qui aura fort peu étudié. Cet homme s'emparera des opinions, des circonstances de la fortune; et il dira du grand théoricien ce que l'architecte praticien disait devant les Athéniens de l'architecte orateur; ce que mon rival vous a dit, je l'exécuterai.»[1]

In these words Guibert, one of the ablest military-writers of his day, predicted the coming of the great Napoleon, and perhaps few prophecies have received more prompt or more startling realization.

They describe Napoleon to the letter—he had not studied much; using words in their ordinary sense, and reducing the thoughts they convey to relative values; he had not thought much, he never had time for that; he had simply

---

1. Then will arise a man, hitherto lost in the obscurity of the crowd; a man who has not made his name either by speech or writing. A man who has meditated silently, and ignoring his own talent, has only been conscious of its power whilst actually exercising it; one who has studied but very little. This man will seize hold of opinions of circumstances and of fortune, and will say of the great theoretician what the practical architect said of the orator, 'All that my rival tells you, I will carry out.'»—Guibert, *Traité de grand Tactique,* 1778.

"done things." Then, from that time forward, the problem has continued to vex men's minds, What was the true secret of his power of execution?

For the eighty years or thereabouts after his downfall at Waterloo, no glimmer of a solution was discovered. Even the acuteness of a mind like that of the keenest military critic which the nineteenth century produced, *viz.*, Clausewitz, failed to shed light on the Napoleonic secret, and the deeds of his most distinguished pupil, von Moltke, show no signs of its appreciation. Napoleon's own comments on his campaigns, dictated, as they mostly are, with the desire to justify his conduct from the standpoint of his own contemporaries, seemed the most barren in suggestion of any, and it was not until the collective intelligence of the whole French General Staff was brought to bear upon his correspondence and the archives which till recently had remained locked up within the walls of the War Ministry in Paris, that it became possible to reconstruct an outline of the train of reasoning which so often led him to victory. This reconstruction explains in the most remarkable manner the true solution of the ethical problem which the persistence of war, "as an act of human intercourse," (to quote Clausewitz's definition) has always involved.

But this solution still leaves us face to face with a psychological problem of extreme interest, that finds its completest expression in the incidents of this campaign of 1813, for it reveals to us Napoleon at his best and at his worst, and compels us to face the question whether he himself was at all times conscious of his own secret—or, in other words, were his successes the outcome of mental processes, or did they spring from impulses of intuitive genius? Was the mind that executed the brilliant manœuvres which culminated on the field of Lützen the same as that which remained hesitating in pitiful indecision during the crisis of events around Dresden, and then again rose to a climax of grandeur in the movements by which he finally brought a nearly two to one numerical superiority on to the decisive point of the battlefield of Leipzig?

The great difficulty to the student of the present day in studying these campaigns is to form an adequate mental picture of the nature of the troops opposed to one another, their courage, intelligence and aptitude for War generally. Progress in armaments and scientific inventions applicable to War has been so vast during the century that has since elapsed that we are apt to lose sight of the fact that, though education of the masses is certainly higher, the ultimate nature of the man has varied very little indeed, and it is this which counts most essentially in War. On the other hand, the means of controlling the masses and generating the "resultant thought wave" which sways alike both armies and crowds, have enormously increased. Where during the Napoleonic epoch it took months, even years, to lash a whole nation into full fighting fury, the Press nowadays can electrify an Empire widespread even as ours into frenzy, and the point of psychological interest is this, that once individuals are united into "crowds" either by contiguity or by community of sentiment, which is ascertained and communicated by the electric telegraph, to say nothing of other more subtle sympathetic currents of forces less generally recognized though equally real, the ultimate unit of the crowd ceases to be a free agent, and becomes an automaton directed and controlled by the will of the majority, almost to the same extent as if he were actually hypnotized; his courage and endurance are increased or diminished far beyond the limit of his own individual will. No average man alone could act with the cowardice of which a panic-struck mob is capable, nor could he rise to the sublime height of self-devotion a well-led assaulting column on a breach has often displayed. Look at the mere physical obstacles such men have overcome in cold blood, and judge by your own feelings. Empirically this fact has always been recognized, and military discipline with all its forms and ceremonies is the direct consequence of centuries of such experience. Its object is to control and regulate such manifestations of the "resultant thought wave," and to ensure that it acts in the direction of self-sacrifice, not of self-preservation. This art of raising men collectively above the fear of death may be considered to have reached its highest development in the days of Frederick the Great. Certainly troops of his nation have never shown equal endurance since; but he had both war-experienced men, time, and physically adequate men to train.

Napoleon had neither time nor really suitable material to work upon, for the Revolution and the years of previous famine had lowered the physical standard of the race, and his officers, though war-experienced, had been trained to a different standard.[1] Hence he had to find means to win battles with inferior troops, and this problem he solved, first by the strategical concentration of greater numbers, and second by a more skilful combination of the three arms, more particularly of the artillery, which had at length developed mobility sufficient for his requirements. In Frederick the Great's day battles had been essentially infantry duels, in which the cavalry intervened at the decisive moment. Under Napoleon the infantry to whom the decisive attack was committed were held back until, as in a siege, the approaches and breaching batteries had so far disturbed the equilibrium, that no serious resistance to the storming columns could any longer be anticipated. His infantry carried position after position, not because they were intrinsically braver than their adversaries, but because, when the time came to launch them forward, they were good enough to face such punishment as their exhausted opponents were still in a condition to administer. Naturally this is not the view the French Infantry took of it. On the contrary,

---

1. Contrast the losses during the battles of the Seven Years' War and those in the encounters of the French Revolution. Average of the principal battles in the former, 17 per cent, in the latter, about 3 per cent.

they were taught to consider themselves irresistible with the bayonet, as, indeed, all infantries must believe themselves to be. Whether they are so or not depends on the skill of the leader who employs them, in suiting the task to their quality; and when that leader fails to grasp the true point, *viz.*, that it is the previously acquired fire superiority, whether of infantry or of artillery, or of both, that determines success, the results are generally disastrous, as in the American Civil War and the Bohemian campaign.

When our own troops are called upon again for a Great War on the Napoleonic scale (and such a war must be the inevitable outcome of the struggle for commercial supremacy now in progress around us), we shall find ourselves very much in the position of the French Generals of the Revolutionary era, *viz.*, with immense numbers of relatively untrained men driven by starvation behind them, and the problem will be how to make the best use of the spirit of self-sacrifice which these men will bring with them, as the necessary consequence of their coming forward at all. Such a War will be very different indeed from any of which the present generation has had direct experience, the only thing that can with certainty be predicted about it being that since it must be fought out under Western conditions of civilization—roads, railways, telegraphs, etc.—it will approximate far more closely to modern French and German conceptions, which are in turn the outcome of the study of the Napoleonic period—than to any more recent model, such as the magnified police raid into the Transvaal, or the eighteenth Century methods forced upon the Japanese by the roadless condition of Manchuria.

Now the cardinal point of the Napoleonic strategy, the spirit underlying the form in which it found expression, was his doctrine of the "economy of forces," which merely meant that every body of troops committed under fire, whether tactically or strategically did not signify, had to be fought out to its utmost limit of endurance. There was no talk in the old Grand

Army of troops being "sacrificed," because every rank knew that self-sacrifice was exactly what their leader expected of them—what they were there for, in fact—because it was only by this sacrifice on their part that he could save up really fresh intact troops for the final act of decision. Generals were strictly called to account by him, if they wasted their men by tactical incompetence; but the spirit of his Army never allowed the men to think for themselves that their chief individual pre-occupation should be "to live to fight another day."

Once this idea is allowed to take root in an Army it always takes a long time and much unnecessary loss of life to eradicate it. Witness the early attempts at battle fighting in the French Revolution and in the American Civil War. It takes many defeats before a whole Army comes to realize that no decisive victories have ever been won by the uncontrolled prowess of individual skirmishers alone; but once it has been learnt, experience shows that even battalions formed of nine-tenths sixty day conscripts, or raw illiterate farmer lads, such as were the East Prussian and Silesian Landwehr, can be trusted to charge home with bayonets and pike in the teeth of the case fire from many batteries, i.e. against a storm of bullets greater by far than any line of breechloaders has ever yet delivered in action; and whether this sacrifice of life has been futile or the reverse has depended, and always will depend, on the skill of the General who ordered it, whether he has correctly seized his opportunity or rashly anticipated it.

It seems to me that, especially with troops of very short service, it is far more imperative to cherish this desire to get killed than the reverse, and fortunately it is the easier of the two to obtain, for all men love the excitement of a charge, even if it is only a mimic one. The newspapers may tell them next day that they would all have been dead men, and that in face of modern weapons, etc., etc., such things are impossible; but they don't believe what they read—perhaps some of the others might have fallen, but not they individually; and there is always the recollection of the wild excitement of the last rush forward, the hoarse roar of cheering from thousands of throats, that brings home, to them what it means to be one with a "crowd" and feel its irresistible forward impulse, to be remembered and talked over.[1]

With the men of the intelligence we now obtain it would seem to me easy to find a way out, of our difficulties, provided our officers are saturated by education with the true spirit of the old time fighting, and understand that bloodshed is a necessary consequence of all armed encounters, and that the degree of it, depends finally on the skill with which the supreme Commander prepares the way for the final decision. Then we can go back to the fundamental proposition on which all the old drill-books were based, *viz.*, that *all* prescribed movements can be carried out on the battle field, that it rests with the judgment of the leader which one to employ in each case as it arises, and that absolute obedience must be rendered to him, because he alone can overlook the whole situation; at any rate no one else can be in an equally good position to do so.

Then bring home to them the peculiarities of the fighting best adapted for each of the successive stages of a great battle. The careful preliminary skirmishing—to cover the advance to the first fire position—the fire preparation in each of its successive stages, and lastly, the final assault, rally and pursuit, when by a combination of artillery and infantry fire the fire superiority has been definitely acquired. The men are mute intelligent enough to appreciate the difference in their lead-

---

1. The real reason why both in the cavalry and infantry the practice of charging in peace fell into disuse was because during the long peace after Waterloo promotion became very slow, and the officers grew too old and infirm to keep their lead in front of the men; they got jostled about by young excited recruits, and very naturally disliked it very much. Some twenty-five years ago it was considered by many cavalry officers as a quite unheard-of thing lo practise the "charge," as they said it unsteadied the horses, whereas the only way to "steady" the horses is to make them gallop together so constantly that they find nothing unusual about the process to get excited about.

ing each of these stages requires, and would enjoy their camps very much more if each ended up with a little excitement, and above all the concentration of really formidable masses. No one who has taken part in the rush of 10,000 men is likely to forget the sensation.

This is the real cause of the extraordinary popularity of the great manoeuvres on the Continent. In anticipation every one dreads the terrible fatigues and the downright suffering often entailed on the men by the tremendous marching, but it all vanishes in the glow of enthusiasm evoked by the final charges on the last days; and the men march back to their quarters or their homes, proud of the fatigues they have over-come, and still throbbing with the excitement of the last few hours. I have seen it both in France, Germany and England, and it is indeed a well-established psychological fact.

In conclusion, let me call attention to the genesis of this little book in my own mind. I spent the early years of my life in Germany, in districts which had been repeatedly over-run by the French Armies, and heard from the lips of the survivors—sufficiently numerous in the early sixties of the last century—what the great struggle for German liberation had meant to them. In 1893 I began collecting material for a study of the period, but learning in Berlin that the whole of the Archives were then being investigated by the General Staff with a view to the preparation of an authoritative his-tory of those times, I abandoned my plan for the moment; and only resumed it again lately when the reorganization of our own forces, and the discussion which has grown up in connection with it, seemed to me to render it advisable to call attention to what has been done under pressure of necessity by other nations, and to show the kind of heroism of which troops fighting for their very existence have been capable of in the not far distant past. Death was the same in those days as it is now, and wounds many times worse; whilst the losses from disease and privation were greater by far than any we

have had to encounter of recent years, except in the East. Yet
these raw levies, averaging less service than our own militia
and volunteers, as they actually stood a few weeks ago, sufficed by their self-devotion to completely neutralize and defeat
the greatest concentration and perhaps the finest tactical feat
of the greatest General of modern times. Want of space pre-
vents my including a complete bibliography of the whole period dealt with, and, moreover, it can be found in many other
places already; but the following are the most recent works
on the subject, and are those which I have more particularly
followed—

Geschichte der Novel Armee im Jahre, 1813. Genl. von
Quistorp.

Geschichte des Frühjahrsfeldzuges, 1813. General von Holleben, 1904.

Geschichte des Herbstfeldzuges, 1813. Major Friedrich,
1906.

Kriegsgeschichtliche Einzelstudien herausgegeben vom
Grossen Generalstabe.

*Urkundliche Beiträge und Forschungen zur Geschichte des
Preussischen Heeres.* (Generalstab.)

Bautien. Col. Foucarb, Paris, 1901.

La Manœuvre de Lützen. Col. de Lanrezac.

L'Education Militaire de Napoléon. Colin, Paris, 1901.

CHAPTER 1

The Prussian Army in 1813

In the struggle for the survival of the fittest amongst the Nations, ever in progress around us, and of which "War" is the name we apply to its most intense manifestation, the battlefield is the last Court of Appeal. Its decision is for the time being final, and it is right that it should be so, for each Army as it stands facing the other is the ultimate expression of the ethical right of the Nation it represents to continue to exist. Its numbers reflect the spirit of its race, its skill the sense of duty guiding that spirit, and its equipment in every detail reveals the standard of probity guiding the daily relations of its individual units. Is the Nation high-spirited? then its soldiers will be numerous and willing; is its sense of duty high? they will be well trained, well led, and ready to die at their Commander's word; is the standard of honesty high, then they will be well fed, and there will be no cartridges loaded with sawdust in their pouches, and no brown paper soles on their boots.

History sufficiently proves the truth of these elementary propositions and their converse, and it is precisely because military theory has so consistently neglected them in the past that its conclusions for so long have failed to commend themselves to the common-sense of our countrymen, whose own evolution has impressed upon them, often with dramatic intensity, the absurdity of the contention that the fate of Nations can be reduced to a question of the relations of angles, bases and the counting of heads.

For this reason the student of a campaign should set himself to acquire, as a first step in his task, as complete a knowledge as possible of the nature of the two contending forces, and the circumstances which conditioned their growth. It is not enough to be able to write down with accuracy the exact number of men, horses and guns each Commander may have had available at a particular time or place; the essential thing is to realize whether, having regard to the composition and previous history of his command, the General had a right to expose his men at that time and place to the risks which hostile collision invariably entails. Given two Armies of approximate mental equality marching to meet one another from parallel bases (and it is always the first care of a General to make his base parallel to that of his adversary, whatever the relations of the imaginary lines indicating his frontier may be,) then neither can manoeuvre so as to threaten his adversary's communications without exposing his own, nor can he endeavour to surround his enemy without running the risk of seeing his own Army cut in two. One risk or the other, one or both Commanders must accept to bring about a result at all, but the result alone decides whether or not they were justified in accepting the risk.

This result, however, depends, as already pointed out, on the relative fighting value of the two Armies, and since this relation may vary from year to year, oven from hour to hour, it is sufficiently apparent that every human being will seek to guarantee himself against the chance of proving mistaken in his estimate by discovering some method which will ensure a sufficient margin of superior force (moral, material or numerical) at a point of his own selection.

If his enemy will only remain perfectly still, as he does, for instance, in a permanent fortress, or in less degree in an entrenched position, the solution is simple and can be applied with almost unfailing regularity time after time, as in the formal attack of an old-fashioned fortress in Vauban's days. But the matter assumes a totally different aspect when the enemy is free to move also, and the difficulty increases till it becomes insurmountable when your adversary can maintain an average rate of speed about twice as great as your own.

Now this is precisely what occurred during the period of hostilities which culminated in the Seven Years' War. The Prussians, handled by a single resolute man responsible to no one but himself, gained the time their adversaries spent in making up their minds, and devoted it to marching. As the whole ethical standard of their Nation was intrinsically high, the King could exact a correspondingly higher standard of training and discipline from his men, hence when the two Armies met numerical superiority was no longer required along the whole front of battle, but the result could be obtained by local superiority only. This was the origin of Frederick the Great's "oblique" order, and when once a succession of victories had been won by the Prussians, because they kept the spirit of this form before their minds' eyes, (in practice the letter was never quite realised), the Austrians became more and more cautious, and taking to entrenchments to avoid the risk of surprise always threatening them through the greater mobility of the Prussians, the task of the latter became ever easier until the idea was stereotyped throughout their Army, that it was the form of the manoeuvre which decided, and not the fighting.

This idea brought others, equally detrimental to true efficiency, in its train. The success of the manœuvres ultimately depended on the superior fighting quality of that body of troops which came first into contact with the enemy. If, for instance, the Austrians at *A*. shot straighter and faster than their assailants,

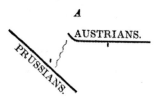

the latter's line would be broken through, no matter what its length (or in other words, its numbers), and through this gap cavalry might pour and work what mischief it pleased. To remedy this the idea of the "échelon" arose, for in this formation it is evident that the units not directly affected by the attack would still remain under control, and this being an obvious improvement on the original model, it took root in the minds of the many, and became a veritable shibboleth of victory.

In either case, however, since it was clearly impossible to predict in advance on which particular unit of the force the brunt of the fighting was to fall, it followed that the excellence of each unit in the essential task of man killing, i.e. the delivery of the most rapid fire from the greatest number of muskets, and the bayonet attack, came to be looked upon as of far greater importance in the decision than superiority of numbers.

To attain the standard of excellence held to be requisite to fulfil these requirements took a great deal of time, and also limited the recruiting area, for men, say of 5ft. 2in., were out of place in a bayonet charge. Hence the finished soldier became a most valuable article, representing, in fact, so much invested capital, and it was clearly poor economy to waste him by unnecessary hardships on the march and in bivouacs, or to impair his resisting power by subjecting him to short rations or inferior food.

Hence the idea sprang up that tents and heavy provision trains were absolute essentials for a mobile Army[1.]

Frederick the Great during the Seven Years' War never allowed himself to be hampered by any such sentiments. When, as after Rossbach (November 5, 1757), the need demanded it, he marched his men to Leuthen as light and as fast as ever did

---

1. Runjit Singh exactly hit off the prevailing sentiment when, on seeing the British Infantry after the first Sikh War in 1840, he said: „Ah, if I had such soldiers as yours, I would have every man carried to the battlefield in palanquins," to prevent their being unnecessarily fatigued before the fighting began.

Napoleon, living on the country as he went. But, as already mentioned, he was responsible to nobody, and possessed in addition that magnetic quality common to all Great Commanders of being able to exact the utmost from his troops without impairing their devotion to his cause. His subordinates, however, were responsible to him, a very different matter, and when after the Peace of Hubertusberg it suited his internal policy to favour commerce and agriculture at the expense of military efficiency, the idea of few but efficient units, of tents and creature comforts, got completely the upper hand in the Army, and the true secret of Prussia's salvation at the crisis of Leuthen, *viz.*, mobility, not the échelon attack, sank into complete obscurity. That the King's policy with regard to Prussian trade and industry was a necessity is clearly evident to anyone who can realize the state of destitution to which the country had been brought during these seven years of incessant strain. Unfortunately, concessions once made to trade and industries are not easily withdrawn, and though the Nation, being mainly dependent on its agriculture, recovered its wealth within seven years—agricultural countries generally do—the system which had sprung into existence in the meanwhile was continued long after the need for it had disappeared, and the efficiency of the Army, more particularly of the Cavalry, was sacrificed to a cheese-paring policy of economy, to which the worst we have ever known was comparatively spendthrift lavishness.

All this took place so gradually that it passed unnoticed by all but the keenest minds.

The system of recruiting for the King's Army (for it was the "Army of the King" and not of the Nation,) was essentially the same as our own, and had, in fact, sprung from the same feudal principles. In theory every man could be called on to serve in defence of his own district, but practically the liability had been commuted for a money payment, with which the King maintained a voluntary Army to defend the country.

Commercially it paid better to attract foreign recruits than to take the physical pick of the country (5ft. 6in. was the minimum height in those days) from the tillage of the fields. In a sense the raising of regiments was decentralized, each district (canton) being liable for a certain quota of men, which it had to supply by ballot, if necessary, and as a general rule no unit was allowed to enlist more than one-third foreigners (*Ausländer*—a term which included all except Prussian subjects), the remaining two-thirds being *"Landeskinder,"* or natives, and it was the presence of these foreigners in the ranks that constituted the gravest evil. These men were easy enough to handle in War, but being long-service men far too proficient in their drill to be kept upon the parade ground, they became idle, and needed an iron hand to keep them in the necessary subjection. They were hated by the civilians, partly for their idleness and the habits they developed as a consequence of that idleness, but chiefly because they corrupted the bulk of all the *"Landeskinder"* who came to the barracks, and every town of sufficient importance to make its voice heard by the King petitioned, and often successfully, to be exempted from their garrison, and to have its inhabitants excused from military service. As each fresh petition was granted, the area for recruiting was diminished, and the rift between the soldiers and civilians, which was to prove the ruin of the country, was gradually widened.

The natural reaction in favour of peace after a period of prolonged War was at its height when the moral storm centre, which culminated in the cataclysm of the Revolution, developed over France, and communicated a fresh impulse to the activity of the peace parties in the towns. These, as the seats of learning and journalistic enterprise, became in turn fresh centres of infection, and presently a wave of sickly humanitarianism overspread the whole of Prussian society, penetrating even into the Army itself, which had already been rendered susceptible to the poison by its bloodless campaign in Bohemia. The situation was best summed up in Rüchel's speech commemorating Prince Henry of Prussia's career in the Army, in which he extolled him in the following words: *Glücklicher als Caesar bei Dyrachium, als Condé bei Rocroi, gewann er ohne Schlacht den Sieg.* And if a General with Rüchel's fighting record could enunciate sentiments like these, it can be imagined to what depths the Peace at any Price party could descend.

Briefly, these views would have done credit to our present day Hague Conference fanatics. War was a barbaric method of settling disputes between rival governments, with which the honest citizen could have no concern, and if it should arise, then private property was to be duly respected and arrangements made to carry it out with the least interference with business matters possible.

These views were common to the whole of Europe at the outbreak of the French Revolutionary Wars, and fundamentally conditioned the whole series of defeats suffered by the Allies during the years 1792-3 and 4, for none of the Nations felt the necessity for great sacrifices or realized the dangers with which they were about to be confronted.

The sequence of cause and effect was, moreover, so obvious to the several Armies engaged, that none of them saw in their defeats a sufficient reason for the sacrifices entailed by the wide-sweeping military reforms which (as subsequent events were to demonstrate) would have been absolutely necessary to ensure their survival.

Indeed, from a military standpoint the soldiers were absolutely right, for locally the superiority of the line tactics copied from the Frederickian model had been abundantly justified. Defeat arose essentially from commissariat and transport difficulties, from which the French, by reason of their poverty, had been compelled to emancipate themselves. All the War Offices were bombarded by advice and proposals for reform, identical in spirit, often even in words, to those with which we in England became so familiar after the Boer War. But out of all these German reformers, only one, Scharnhorst, then in the Hanoverian Army, saw the true cause of all their troubles, namely that the French Revolution had called a new factor into being, the spirit of the "Nation in Arms."[1]

In the absence of this spirit in Prussia lay the root cause of all her subsequent misfortunes. The idea that the Prussian Army had fallen asleep on its laurels is entirely untenable. On the contrary, in no Army in the world had more men devoted themselves to the study of the higher branches of their profession, or was the daily routine work of maintaining the efficiency of the troops carried out with greater fidelity and precision.

Nor was this labour entirely devoted to "spit and polish", as it is the custom to believe. On the contrary, the diaries of regimental officers and other contemporary documents recently published by the German General Staff[2] record a succession of experimental field days, days on the ranges, mornings spent in packing wagons, testing camp gear, etc., that remind one most forcibly of months spent on the Indian Frontier, where at least no one has accused the British officer of "slacking." But the resemblance goes deeper here than is at first obvious, because, in neither case was the spirit of the people prepared to make the necessary financial sacrifices; in both, nine-tenths of the energy was wasted for want of proper material to work upon.

The very foundation of an officer's training for higher commands lies in his power of bending human nature to his will, and the development of that will by constant clash and friction with the wills of others. A man learns more in licking a raw company of recruits into shape in six weeks, than in doing duty with a made battalion in as many years.

Compulsory service in Prussia could alone have given the officers material to work upon. But though the matter

---

1. *Die Ursachen unsere Niederlagen in den Niederlanden*, 1794.
2. *Urkundliche Forschungen zur Geschichte des Prussischen Heeres,* Berlin, 1902-4.

was discussed from every point of view and Knesebeck's memorandum[1] foreshadowed almost exactly the steps ultimately taken, and for which the credit is unanimously assigned to Scharnhorst, (although he died of wounds received at Bautzen the year before they were actually embodied in the law), the truth was, that the People were not ready for any sacrifice involving either their personal freedom, or their pockets. Further than this, though parliamentary control in Prussia was non-existent, public opinion nevertheless had ways of making itself felt, which no crowned head could afford to neglect. Hence, since no increase in the estimates could be entertained on any account, absolutely pressing reforms costing money could only be carried through by robbing Peter to pay Paul. There were, however, a great many Peters, and a great many Pauls, each of whom had vested interests which could not be hampered without creating friction which it required lubrication to overcome. That lubrication was always found by an extension of the system of furloughs and of "watch free" men, and this struck at the very basis of efficiency.

That Frederick the Great was well aware of this evil is apparent from the speech he made at one of his last Cavalry inspections held at Potsdam.

> Gentlemen, I am entirely dissatisfied with the Cavalry. The Regiments are completely out of hand; there is no accuracy in their movements, no solidity, no order. The men ride like tailors. I beg that this may not occur again, and that each of you will pay more attention to his duty, more particularly to the horsemanship.
>
> But I know how things go on. The Captains think only of making money out of their Squadrons, and the Lieutenants, how to get the most leave. You think I am not up to your dodges, but I know them all and will

---

1. See von der Goltz's *Roszbach und Jena.*

36

recapitulate them. Tomorrow, when you start on your march back to your garrison, before you are ten miles on your way, the Squadron Commander will ask the Sergeant-Major whether any of the men live in the vicinity, and the Sergeant-Major will reply, 'Yes, sir; there are —— and —— live quite close to here, and will be glad to go on furlough.' 'Very well then,' the Captain will say, 'we can save their pay.[1] Send the names in to me tonight, and they shall have leave.' And so it goes on every march. The Lieutenants get leave to visit their friends, and the Captain arrives at his garrison with half the Squadron leading the horses of the other half, like a band of disreputable Cossacks.

Then when the season for riding drills comes on, the Captain sends for the Sergeant-Major, and says: 'I have an appointment this morning at —— and must get away early; tell the first Lieutenant to take the rides.' So the Sergeant-Major goes to the first Lieutenant and gives him the message, and the latter says: 'What! the Captain is away. Then I am off hunting. Tell the second Lieutenant to take the men.' And the second Lieutenant, who is probably still in bed, says:

'What! both of them gone! Then I shall stay where I am; I was up till 3 this morning at a dance; tell the Cornet I am ill, and he must take the rides.' And the Cornet says: 'Look here, Sergeant-Major, what's the good of my standing out there in the cold? You know all about it much better than I do; you go and take the rides.' And so it goes on. And what must be the end of it all?

Now march your Regiments home, and don't let me have to speak like this again.[2]

---

1. The money went into the contingent allowance, thence indirectly to the Captain's pocket.
2. *Aus meinem Tagebuch, von Martwitz*. See also *Cavalry Past and Future* by the Author.

But neither he nor his successors were able to suggest a remedy, and the result was that at the time of the Jena campaign the evil had reached such dimensions that nearly two-thirds of the whole strength of the Army—that is to say, almost the whole of the *Landeskinder* contingent served only for *one month* in the year, and when it is remembered how infinitely more complicated the whole drill and training of the soldier was in those days as compared to our own time, one can only marvel at the devotion of the permanent staff who succeeded in this short period in getting such precision in movement and discipline in the field (out of such almost hopeless material) as the battlefields of Jena and Auerstädt undoubtedly proved them to possess. Unfortunately this work fell essentially on the non-commissioned officers, and not on the officers, as it should have done.

Nevertheless, the troops were, according to the standard of the period, well found in every respect, (except in great coats,)[1] and many important reforms, such as the introduction of light infantry battalions, of improved muskets, of rifles for the picked shots of each company, the provision of a small reserve of trained men to meet the first losses of a campaign; and, last but not least, the formation of independent Divisions of all arms on the French model were actually carried into effect.

This last deserves a paragraph by itself, for though unquestionably right in principle, a defect in its execution proved practically the determining causes of the final disaster at Jena.

---

1. The want of great coats arose in the following manner. In the chronic wars at the beginning of the 18th century the men wore a long-waisted, sleeved waistcoat; over this a substantial frockcoat, which came down to the knee and was folded back when marching. This cut into a great deal of cloth, and when peace came, the Colonels having the clothing contract found they could economize money by skimping their men's coats, so that by degrees the frockcoat shrank to a ridiculous coatee about as warm as the old waistcoat, which disappeared altogether. Then it was discovered that the men's health suffered through such insufficient clothing, and "watchcoats" for sentry-go were introduced, and it was intended to introduce these for the whole Army when the War broke out.

This defect lay in splitting up the whole of the Cavalry and Artillery and distributing them approximately equally to the Infantry commands. The consequence was that both arms lost the habit of working in "masses," and "masses" under the hand of the Army Commander were absolutely essential to counter the tactics of the French Army. Fifty squadrons under a Seydlitz at Auerstädt, or a hundred guns under a Senarmont at Jena, might have changed the fate of Europe; but no such men were forthcoming, and one of the most gallant Armies of which history has any record was destroyed in driblets, because it lacked a firm skeleton of force to hold the fractions together.

On the afternoon of October 14, 1806, upon the plains of Jena the Army of Frederick the Great ceased to exist, and only scattered fragments drifted away north and west, without plan, or any design for reunion.[1] They had been beaten, not through any fundamental defect in their tactical training. *It is necessary to insist on that,* but, in so far as any purely military reason can be assigned for their fate, it was because their Generals, grown old in the traditions of the Seven Years' War had never realized that the mobility of an Army is not so much a question of how fast men can swing their legs along a road, but of how long it takes their leaders to decide along which roads they shall march. Never before or since has the fate of a Nation depended so wholly on what men generally call chance, but which some of us prefer to attribute to the direct interposition of the Almighty, to whom, after all, public opinion still attributes the position of Arbitrator of the Battlefield.

When morning broke on that fateful day, a dense fog, seemingly not anticipated by anyone on the field, (though after all

---

1. This collapse, however, was an absolutely necessary outcome of the false conception of War which had sprung up from the false humanitarianism of the age. War was a curse and an anachronism having no place in its enlightened philosophy. The soldier was a useless drone, living on the hard-earned savings of the honest citizen, and the outcome of these opinions was the tyranny of France in Germany, after the disastrous battle of Jena.—See *Voluntary and Compulsory Service,* also *War and the World's Life,* by the Author.

a very frequent phenomenon on an October morning) hung low over the whole plateau, on which the Prussians stood, and it was thanks to that accident alone that the French Emperor, Lannes and the Imperial Guard escaped annihilation. It is utterly inconceivable that had the Prussians been able to see their target of 50,000 men crowded in a dense mass, each one pressing breast against the knapsack of the man in front of him, on the narrow summit of the Landgrafenberg, they could have failed to seize their opportunity. Had they done so, with the Guard, Lannes, and the Emperor routed, neither Ney, Augereau, or Bernadotte were the men to have saved the situation.

After Jena there followed a series of consequences, the absolutely inevitable results which must everywhere ensue when a Nation, having lost touch with the realities of life, forgets that War is a necessary incident in its evolution which cannot be evaded by refusing to recognize its existence. The Prussian people, believing the question at issue to be solely the affair of Governments and their instruments (the Armies), welcomed the conquerors as deliverers, and turned their own soldiers, even the wounded, away from their doors with an excess of brutality which disgusted even the French troops, whose previous experience had rendered them anything but squeamish on the score of humanity.

The Prussian Generals, trained for a whole generation to a blind veneration for civil law and the sacred rights of private property, did not dare to accept the responsibility of requisitioning the food and shelter of which their men stood so urgently in need. They left the ample resources which the country afforded to fall into the hands of the French, who were restrained by no such pusillanimous scruples. But it was not hunger alone that led to the wholesale surrenders characteristic of this phase of the War. The retreat was in fact the very converse of that of the French five years later from Russia, when hunger brought about the complete disruption of the bonds of discipline, and those fractions of the Army which still held together owed their salvation solely to the unconquerable spirit of their Chiefs. Here the German troops stuck to their ranks until they fell from sheer exhaustion. It was the Leaders who betrayed the honour of their men, not through intentional treachery or cowardice (their subsequent records, as we shall see hereafter, abundantly clear them of that dishonour), but because they too had become inoculated with that *false humanitarianism which places the individual above the race*—and in its short-sightedness is ready to purchase immediate relief at the cost of enhanced suffering for the many hereafter.

A perfect epidemic of surrender set in amongst the higher Commanders—not only did detachments in the open field lay down their arms by order, but Commandants of fortresses, such as Magdeburg, Cüstrin, Torgau and Spandau opened their gates unconditionally, "to avert the further suffering of the civil population."

As von der Goltz has explained in his *Von Jena bis Preussische Eylau,* current military opinion, founded mainly on the events of the latter years of Frederick's life, had led Prussian Generals to look on War more as an intellectual exercise than as the direction and control of elemental forces.

You played the game according to the rules, and when the rules indicated that you had lost, you submitted with a good grace and cheered the winner, like the crew of a beaten yacht after a race. Only Blücher and Scharnhorst, who being thrown together during the retreat, learnt to know and appreciate each other's characters, seem to have stood out resolutely against the general trend of sentiment, and their chance association was destined to bear remarkable fruit in years to come.

Meanwhile most of Pomerania and all East Prussia escaped for the moment the ravages of the invaders, and when on November 5, the last remnants of the Field Army passed into captivity, there still remained available, according to von der Goltz, trained men enough to place some 40 battalions and 55 squadrons in the field. But instead of calling these out to

41

the last man and horse, the talk at the Royal Headquarters was only of peace, and peace there probably would have been but for the Emperor Alexander, who, untroubled by the fate of his Ally, determined to continue his war with Napoleon, and Napoleon's own excessive demands, which simply drove King Frederick William IV into the arms of the Russians.

Ultimately, when all hope of pacifying the Emperor by further surrender was at an end, a small field force of some 12,000 men was mobilized and sent to join the Russians. These, by their timely arrival on the field of Preussische Eylau, succeeded in averting the complete defeat of the Russian Army, and by the relative ease with which they had driven the exhausted remnants of the Divisions under St. Hilaire and Friant before them, they brought the first gleam of hope to the soldiers of the old Prussian Army. It convinced them that when the time came, under competent leaders, these men could still give an excellent account of themselves even against the victors of Jena.

The treaty of Tilsit on July 9, 25 days after the battle of Friedland, brought the war to an end. After that not a moment was lost in setting to work at the reform and regeneration of the Prussian Army.

A Royal Commission under the presidency of Scharnhorst, with Gneisenau, Boyen and Grolman as members, was assembled on the 25th of the same month at Memel. In January, 1808, it moved to Königsberg, and early in that year produced a report which may be considered as the starting point of the modern German Army, notwithstanding the fact that at the moment Scharnhorst's proposals for universal service were not deemed practicable by the King, and did not in fact become law until September, 1814, nearly a year after that great soldier's death.

By this scheme the Prussian Army was in future to consist of three Corps, based on Prussia, Pomerania and Silesia respectively, with a total field strength of 84 battalions, 96 squadrons and 24 batteries of Artillery.

The distinction between *Ausländer* and *Landeskinder* was done away with. In principle, though voluntary recruiting was maintained, the law compelling "Cantons," or districts, to furnish their allotted contingent of recruits was revised and strengthened. But far too large a number of local privileges with regard to exemption were retained. The whole system of furlough men, and of *Friewächter*[1] was swept away, and it was decreed that in future no Prussian soldier might be subjected to corporal, or other, degrading punishment.

At the same time a Court was appointed to inquire into all cases of surrender of fortresses, or in the open field, before which officers of all ranks were cited to appear. Fortunately procedure and communications were both so slow and uncertain, that only some cases had been dealt with, and none of the death sentences, eight in all,[2] had been carried out, when the general amnesty announced in the King's proclamation to his people accompanying the declaration of War against France on March 16th, 1813, suspended all proceedings.

The actual cadres available for the new Army in December, 1807, amounted to 50 Line Battalions, 11 Companies of Light Infantry, 9 Companies of Rifles and 86 Squadrons (no Batteries are mentioned by Holleben, which indicates the little importance attached to Artillery at the period) but this amount, limited though it was in comparison with Prussia's former power, appeared altogether excessive to Napoleon, who on January 1, 1809, published his celebrated decrees limiting the whole Prussian Field Army to 42,000 men, to be apportioned amongst the three arms as follows—

10 Infantry Regiments		22,000
8 Cavalry Regiments (of 4 Squadrons)		8,000
Artillery and Sappers		6,000
Guard, Infantry and Cavalry		6,000
	Total	**42,000**

---

1. Men exempted from duty and allowed to practise their trades in the town.
2. *See* Lehmann's *Life of Scharnhorst.*

No increase was allowed for the next ten years. This blow came like a thunderbolt upon the reformers, already well advanced in their great undertaking.

The idea of Army Corps, even of Divisions, had to be abandoned, and six Brigades substituted as the principal unit consisting each of 7 to 8 battalions, 12 Squadrons and a Brigade of Artillery, comprising 12 Companies of foot and three of horse artillery—each being armed with 6 guns, 12 or 6-pounders and 2 howitzers.

Scharnhorst also endeavoured to create a "National Guard" on the model of the French organization, but this was vetoed by Napoleon, though he did allow the inhabitants of Berlin and some of the other large towns to organize themselves for the maintenance of order.

All the ingenuity of the Reformers was now devoted to the circumvention of the Napoleonic decree, and many were the expedients resorted to. Amongst others a most promising idea was started for the "relief of the unemployed" by finding them work on the repair of the coast fortresses, always liable to attack from the British Fleet. As most of the unemployed were old soldiers, and as the only decent clothing available for them happened to be the stores of old uniforms; in a surprisingly short time it became indispensable to issue these uniforms, as after even a few days' work, the rags the poor fellows brought with them became a scandal to public morality. Thus some 6 to 7,000 good and true men were kept together who only needed muskets to become most formidable soldiers. But this adroit measure did not escape the eye of the French Emperor, and presently this system was vetoed also.

The chief means of escape from French restrictions was found in the extension of a time-honoured custom of the old Army, by which every military unit had been allowed to entertain a few supernumerary recruits known as *Krümpers* as a part trained reserve against mobilization.

This system was now extended, and each Company, Squadron or Battery was authorized to call up three to four men for one month's training, dismissing them at the end of that time and replacing them by others. But even this seemed superfluous to Napoleon, and the number was finally fixed at eight per Company, and three per Squadron for four months' training.

Fortunately during 1810-11, smuggling in the Baltic reached such a pitch that Napoleon felt it expedient to relax the stringency of his restrictions, and a few more men found employment as coastguards.

In August, 1811, the Prussians had actually 74,000 trained men available, of whom 48,000 belonged to the Field Army.[1] But Napoleon had now determined to force the Prussians to declare war against Russia, and to furnish him with a contingent therefore. Accordingly on September 13, he instructed St. Marsan, his Ambassador to Berlin, to demand the suspension of their preparations and their agreement to join him in his contemplated enterprise, giving the King only three days in which to decide. At the same time he warned Davoût at Hamburg to be ready to move into Prussia at a moment's notice, adding this characteristic instruction as to his behaviour, which advocates of Hague Conferences would do well to remember. *Si vous entrez en Prusse, il ne faut faire aucune proclamation, ni rien dire, mais tout prendre, et désarmer (Corres. 18,139).*

This threat compelled the King to temporize. All preparations in excess of Napoleon's limitations were stopped, and Blücher, Scharnhorst and others to whom the Emperor had taken exception were dismissed. Finally he yielded, and on February 24, 1812, an alliance with France was concluded, by which Prussia agreed to furnish a contingent of 19 Battalions, 24 Squadrons and 60 guns under the command of von Grawert, who was subsequently relieved by von Yorck on August 13 of the same year.

---

1. P. 13. *Holleben*, Vol. I.

There remained then in Prussia, as a nucleus for further formations, 26 Battalions, 54 Squadrons and 108 guns, or 22,394 men, field troops, 9,785 for garrisons, and in the 6,052 depots. The field troops were thoroughly efficient, and, thanks to the particular circumstances under which they had fought at Eylau, had recovered confidence in themselves, which was not weakened by their experiences in Russia; and behind the garrisons and depots there existed a large number of veterans of 1806-7 who had managed to make their way back to their homes, but could not be enrolled owing to the terms of Napoleon's decree, already referred to above.

CHAPTER 2

The French Army in 1813

Up to the outbreak of the French Revolution the French Army had been recruited on a voluntary basis. The power to call out a certain quota of men from each district, to make good any deficiency in the supply of volunteers, existed as in Prussia, but had seldom been enforced, and even after the outbreak of the Revolution the greatest reluctance to enlist men into the Regular Army, except with their own goodwill, was shown. Since numbers, however, had to be found far in excess of the regular Army establishments, all sorts of expedients were attempted. Volunteer regiments were formed and the *levée en masse,* was decreed. Actually, however, law was so completely in abeyance during the first years of this period, that practically all the men who faced the enemy at the front may be considered essentially as volunteers. Whether raised originally by conscription, or joining of their own free will, the men generally began their service by deserting, and when on return to their homes they found their places filled up by others, and starvation or denunciation staring them in the face, they rejoined the colours as on the whole the safest place, and settled down to their soldiering with a fairly good grace. This requires to be understood, as it explains the excellent spirit shown under the greatest hardships and privation by the Armies of the Rhine and of Italy, and accounts in a great measure for the soldierly tone of the troops throughout the following years of. Napoleon's conquest, until the horrors of the retreat from Moscow in 1812 temporarily destroyed all organization.

It was not until 1798 that a regular system of conscription became law in France, and though it was not so rigid as that subsequently adopted by Prussia in 1814 (being more generous in exemptions, and retaining the dangerous system of paid substitutes), yet, incomplete as it was, it formed the whole foundation for Napoleon's subsequent career, for no other ruler in Europe could afford "to expend 30,000 men a month," as he brutally expressed it.

Actually, in order not to make his rule unnecessarily unpopular, Napoleon did not in his early years exercise to its full extent the power which the law conferred upon him. His Allies at that time had to find the bulk of his Army, the French Regiments merely replacing casualties and wastage as they arose; but the men not taken were nevertheless liable for service till their twenty-sixth year, and were thus available to meet any crisis which might arise. Assured of this reserve supply of raw material, the Emperor was free to conceive and practise methods of strategy and tactics to which his adversaries, Austria, England and Prussia, could oppose no reply—because they dared not contemplate (without a certain supply of men to fall back upon) the terrible destruction of troops which his rapid marches and battles entailed. *This is the central feature of the whole period of Napoleonic warfare, and must be kept steadily in mind, if true conclusions from its phenomena are to be drawn.*

Out of the whole Grand Army of some of 600,000 men, who in 1812 crossed the Russian frontier, only 200,000, in round numbers, were of French extraction.[1] The population of France being approximately 36 millions, the annual contingent should have been, in round figures, 360,000 of which at least 180,000 would have been physically fit for service. Hence, making the usual allowance for wastage, and deducting a whole million for

---

1. *See* Max Jähn's *Französische Heer,* also Rousset and the Duke d'Aumale.

men killed and permanently disabled during his campaigns, there should have been in France not less than two and a half million men still of an age to bear arms when Napoleon returned to Paris in January, 1813. The extent to which he fell short of raising these numbers is evidence of the growing unpopularity of his pitiless rule, and of the extraordinary laxity of internal administration. There was, therefore, no real deficiency of men for a new Army, after the calamities of the Russian Retreat, but there was a great want of officers and non-commissioned officers to form cadres around which to group the men.

Fortunately, and possibly in view of the actual eventuality, Napoleon had organized a special body of National Guards, strictly for home defence, during the previous year. To mark distinctly the difference between their status and that of troops of the Regular Army, they had been formed in "cohorts", not in "battalions". As a matter of fact, though there was a distinction there was no difference, for these "cohorts", having been recruited from amongst the better class whose position had secured them the favour of the *préfets* of their districts, and being officered by men who had seen service, had acquired a very fair standard of drill and discipline. Consequently the "cohorts" were at once invited to volunteer as units for the emergency, and since the great majority of their men would have been liable, in case of refusal, to go as conscripts of the previous years, of two evils they accepted the least, and were amongst the first to march for the front, where they did excellent service.

Napoleon's next step was to call out 100,000 men of the contingents of 1808-9-10, who had escaped previous drafts, and then in quick succession the whole contingents for 1813 and 1814, which should have given at least 360,000 men. As a fact they did not realize more than 200,000, so great was the incessant wastage from desertion.[1]

---

1. For details of desertion and measures to stop it, see "Les Refractaires" in supplement to *Mil. Wochblt*, 1887.

To weld this raw material into shape, officers and non-commissioned officers were withdrawn wholesale from the troops in Spain, and as the survivors of the Grand Army drifted back into Germany, all not absolutely required at the front were sent back by post to Mayence, and the Rhine to take up their places in the new units.

As fast as the new recruits arrived at the Depots, they were formed into provisional Companies, about 100 strong, and marched off to the frontiers by ten to fifteen mile stages, picking up arms and uniform, at the arsenals they passed through, and drilling a couple of hours every afternoon. At the frontier these Companies were grouped into provisional Battalions, and again despatched on their way, drilling as they went. As the average number of stages was from forty-five to sixty, with one rest day in five, by the time they reached the front, they had been some sixty to eighty days under arms, were in thorough marching condition, and on the whole were rather better fitted for their work than would be a fair British Militia Battalion at the end of its annual training. The Artillery also reached the front in good condition, the supply of guns and material was ample, though sometimes antiquated in pattern, the supply of draught horses sufficient and of fair quality, and the traditions of the Service quite admirable. The Cavalry and Staff formed the weakest links in the chain. The former had suffered most of all during the Retreat from Moscow, and the supply of riding horses in France, never of a high stamp, had been so exhausted by previous efforts, that thousands of men had to be marched into Germany on foot, and saw their horses for the first time almost in presence of the enemy. British Officers with South African experience can easily picture the consequences of such conditions. Fortunately the demands made on the Staff were not of a high order. With Corps and Divisional Commanders so thoroughly war-trained, little more than courage and goodwill on the part of their assistants was required, and in these qualities the French were never lacking.

A few words are now needed to explain the evolution of the tactical forms which these troops were about to employ. The old Royal Army of France had been trained essentially on Prussian lines, indeed the drill book for the Infantry of 1791 was an adaptation of an edition of the Prussian regulations originally drafted by Guibert, who died before its publication,[1] but though the *form* was the same, the French had never succeeded in assimilating the *spirit*. French national characteristics were all against the extreme rigidity and slowness which characterized the Prussian model, and for years before the Revolution there had existed a school diametrically opposed to the regulation methods. The whole nation took sides in the discussions which followed, the popular side being all against the official attitude, and it happened that the former received very strong corroboration of their principles from the experiences brought back from Canada and the United States by the men who had fought against us in both countries. Moreover, when the great era of revolutionary warfare commenced in 1792, there was obviously no time to train the raw levies called forth by the Revolution to anything approaching the standard of dexterity in loading and manoeuvring which the old time tactics required. A compromise between the two was the only possible solution, and in face of the enemy the French Infantry evolved a working system of its own, based primarily on adaptation of forms to circumstances. In other words, they fought in line when they could, as skirmishers and in columns when they had to, and by the time Napoleon assumed control over them they had become a supple and finished instrument ready to his hand, and needing only the directions of his genius and the driving power of his will to ensure great results.

A further change of far-reaching importance had also evolved itself from the conditions of their growth. It be-

1. See Max Jahns, *Kriegsgeschichtlichen Wissenschaften*, Vol. IV. p. 2,594. Compare also Colin's *Le Discipline et la Tactique dans les Armées de la Révolution.*

ing impossible, in the time available, to create the discipline needed for the rigid order of battle of the Frederickian period, more importance had to be conceded to the personal element of command. The more highly disciplined the troops, the less it appears necessary to consult their likes and dislikes; but raw troops can only be relied on to follow the man whom they trust, and it takes time, more or less according to the personality of the leader, to win this confidence. Hence, *generally, the longer men can be held together under the same Commander, the better is the guarantee for their efficiency.* This led, naturally, to the growth, first of the Division, then of the Corps, as an organic whole, the units of which were kept permanently together till men and officers understood and relied on each other implicitly.

This rendered decentralization of command practicable. Army Headquarters no longer required to issue detailed instructions to every unit in the whole command, but could confine themselves to informing the Commander of the Division or Corps as to the general intention of a manœuvre, and the part which his unit was expected to play in it, leaving it to him to make his own arrangements for carrying out his special task. *Essentially, it was the enormous economy in time, rendered possible by this decentralization, which gave the French Armies their great superiority in mobility over all others, on which in turn the earlier strategy of Napoleon was principally based.*

The growth of the Divisional system led in time to the closer association of the several arms of the service. Infantry, Cavalry and particularly Artillery, learnt to play together, and no longer lost sight of the whole in the pursuit of their own glorification. Thus the Artillery developed in tactical mobility and its officers trained themselves for the part they were destined to play. On the other hand, the Cavalry, no longer being called on to act in masses, lost sight of those essential factors in their training which alone renders possible their action in "mass." In consequence of this they never again found opportunity to make good their shortcomings in this respect. It was want of *horsemanship* primarily, not of *horsemastership* which lay at the root of their many failures.

Unlike Frederick the Great, who devised a system of tactics and then forged the tools to suit it, Napoleon paid little attention to the making of his instruments, his crowded life left him too little opportunity, *but he took the tools ready to his hand and made the best possible use of them as he found them.*

In this, however, he remains the "Master" for all time. But he did not burst full fledged into the Battle world; he grew to his full stature by a process, brief indeed as measured against other great Generals' lives, but presenting, nevertheless, well marked stages which it is imperative to keep in mind.

What was chiefly noticeable about him in his youth was not conspicuous mental capacity, but an astonishing power of command, which he exercised apparently unconsciously, the astounding feature being that even in Corsica, his own country, where prophets are usually held in least respect, men, years his superior in experience, rendered him spontaneous and willing obedience, though under no obligation whatever to do so.

Though Brienne is always spoken of as a military college, in fact there existed at that place no special military curriculum at all—his reading there, and previous to his prolonged leave to Corsica, had been of the most general nature, nor can it be truthfully said that such notes of his as have been handed down to us show any very marked symptoms of unusual genius. It was not until he joined the battalion of the Royal Artillery whose Headquarters were at Valence in 1791 that he appears to have taken up any military study in earnest. Here he came under the influence of a first-rate Artillerist, Baron du Teil, his Commanding Officer, who quickly appreciated his ability, and took him into his confidence. Du Teil was a well-known military authority in his day, and at his house it is probable that Bonaparte met d'Urtubi and Gassendi, all equally eminent in their way. He certainly read the works of Guibert and Feuquiéres, and he could hardly help studying *Lloyd's History of the Seven Years' War.* Marshal Saxe's *Reveries* were also not without influence on him, and he had access to the two works on Mountain Warfare of Bosroger and Bourcet, which were considered so important in those days that they were never printed, but circulated from hand to hand in manuscript copies.[1] The leading characteristic of all these works can be briefly summarized. All were permeated by the *spirit of attack,* all saw clearly that the *decision of the battlefield was everything,* and that Artillery was essentially the arm by whose concentrated action the way could be swept clear for the attacking columns, whether of horse or foot, or both, to penetrate or roll up the enemy's line of resistance.

If the practice of the eighteenth century lagged far behind these principles, this was due to causes inherent in the nature of things, which could only be modified by revolutionary up-heaval, and it was Napoleon's good fortune that he arrived on the scene at the very moment when all the barriers of the past had been swept away, and he was able to employ the means at his disposal without hindrance from the causes which had tied the hands of his predecessors.

His first campaign of 1796 reveals absolutely nothing be-yond what any one of his teachers in the War could them-selves have planned, though all probably would have lacked the astounding energy and power of command which was peculiar to him alone. In the battles east of Milan, his plans were based on the complete pre-eminence of the tools at his disposal, (both in marching and fighting,) over their adversaries—a de Wet might have done as much—and in the Marengo Campaign we find him so over-confident in the fighting qualities of his soldiers, that he threw to the winds all the usual maxims of concentration on the deci-

---

1. See Colin's *Education Militaire de Napoléon,* p. 135, et seq.

sive point, all care for his communications, and was caught at hopeless disadvantage by the Austrians, only escaping disaster by a miracle.

It would seem that it was the Ulm Campaign[1] which first opened his eyes to the possibilities which might arise *if his enemy insisted on doing the wrong thing, or something which from the Emperor's point of view was so utterly preposterous that he had completely failed to provide for such action in his general scheme.*

He crushed Mack, not by strategic prevision, but simply because he was in full and undisputed command of some 200,000 first-rate fighting men, able to march at least twice as far in twenty-four hours as the 80,000 Austrians opposed to them. But for a series of occurrences within the Austrian Army which Napoleon neither could, nor in fact did, foresee, Mack would have escaped his grasp, with consequences for the French Army almost as bad as a defeat in the open field. The spectacle of six French Corps, some 150,000 men, converging on a geographical point devoid of defenders from which all food had been removed or destroyed, would have made the Emperor the laughing stock of Europe, and must have shaken his prestige with his own men to a degree which would have rendered it impossible for him to have called upon them to face again the hunger and privation of a similar march.

At Austerlitz, the enemy attacked him, *hence the central problem of strategy—viz., how to hold fast the enemy and compel him to stand to be beaten*—never arose, and there is no indication in his correspondence, to the best of my knowledge, to show how he would have solved it.

But by the opening of the Jena Campaign,[2] it is clear that he had thought the question out in its entirety, and realized to the full that the *"independent will power"* of the adversary is *after all the most difficult factor to control in war.* His first object was to beat the Prussians thoroughly and decisively, before the

---

1. See *Campaign de 1805,* Alombert et Colin.
2. See Bonnal's *La Manœuvre de Jena.*

Russians could join them, but how if the Prussians refused to stand to be beaten? He calculated, and as the event proved correctly, that a threat at their Capital would be certain to provoke them to attempt its defence. But he could not foresee from which direction his enemy might attempt to interfere with his march thither; hence he resolved to march his troops in such a formation that he would be equally ready to fight him from whatever quarter the attack might come.

This led him to his celebrated "battalion square of 200,000 men." It is the same reasoning, in fact, that has led us to the formation of squares in the Soudan—but with this difference, *which is very essential.*

The French Army had to cover an area big enough to afford subsistence for its men, because it had abandoned the magazine system of Frederick the Great's day, and had also to be adapted to the roads of the district they traversed. Therefore it was impossible to march ready for action literally at a moment's notice, and consequently Advance Guards or Flanking parties had to be sent out, of such strength and to such distances, that their resistance, even if attacked by overwhelming numbers, could gain time for the remainder of the troops to concentrate.

A weak advance, or flank, guard, or one of Cavalry only, might, of course, give warning of the enemy's approach, but it could not *hold* that enemy or hinder him in the execution of his designs; but some sixty thousand men attacking with vigour could not be neglected, and would force the enemy to turn and fight, *thus riveting his attention and creating a fixed point about which the remainder of the assailants could manoeuvre.*

This will be clearer if the accompanying diagram is consulted. Had Lannes and Augereau, for instance, been attacked from the direction of Magdala, by the whole Prussian Army (as might well have happened) they had room to manoeuvre, and even 180,000 Prussians could not have wiped out 60,000 of the best French troops under twenty-four hours' fighting; but in twenty-four hours the remainder of the French Army would have appeared on the field, and victory, generally, is to the Commander who can place the last closed forces on the field. The plan would work equally if the Prussians struck the Advance Guard under Davoût and Bernadotte. The two combined were quite capable of holding their own until the Emperor with the Main body could arrive, and though in fact, the Prussians did neither, but separated their forces on the eve of the engagement, this only weakened their chances of victory as far as the strategic side of the question was concerned. Actually, as we have seen in the previous chapter, the fate of the day turned on the tactical errors of the Prussians. But had Davoût and Bernadotte remained together, as Napoleon evidently anticipated and desired, the arrival of these sixty thousand men even very late in the day might have been counted on to avert disaster, if not defeat.

It is, however, clear that the very readiness for immediate action which this formation implied, renders it certain that Napoleon did not discount the consequences of victory beforehand. Not a detachment was made to threaten the enemy's communications in advance, but the troops *were arranged to win the battle first,* no matter what position relatively to the enemy's possible lines of retreat might result from the fighting. The general conception of strategical manoeuvring common throughout all Europe until his time (and prevailing in some countries even to-day) aimed at reaping the results of victory before the victory itself was won. In fact they tried to "sell the skin before they had killed the bear." As we shall see later on, Napoleon himself sometimes fell into this error, but this was the outcome of his overweening confidence in the power of his troops to win, when fighting under his direct personal control.

From 1806 onward, this tendency *to hold and fix the enemy so as to obtain a pivot about which to manoeuvre became the characteristic of the Napoleonic system.* Even though at times one seems to detect marked divergencies from it, as at Pultusk (1807) in particular, analysis only shows that like the rest of us, the greatest Generals have to bow to the old saying *on fait la soupe avec ce qu'on a, non avec ce qu'on veut,* and roads and conditions of supply at times proved stronger than his desire.

From the clutch of this system no enemy could escape unless endued with superior mobility and greater staunchness combined, for only troops of the highest order could endure the strain of repeated retreats without dissolution. Moreover, it was necessary for these tactics of evasion that the theatre of operations should have ample depth, as in Russia, and this depth was not always forthcoming. It is in the successive variations of these factors that the strategic interest of the Campaign of 1813 principally lies.

Meanwhile tactical evolution had also been at work, to which it is now necessary briefly to refer.

The strength of the old Revolutionary Army had lain, as already pointed out, in its admirable Infantry and its Divisional system, and it was essentially with the «turning movements» these two factors facilitated, that Napoleon won his victories up to the time of Jena and Friedland. But after the horrors of the Campaign in Poland the spirit of the French Infantry began to deteriorate, whilst at the same time their opponents not only became more numerous, but the temperature of their fighting spirit steadily rose. The whole problem of battle-leading now resolved itself into this *"How to create conditions which would render it possible for the Infantry, such as it was, to advance at all,"* and Macdonald's Corps at Wagram[1] shows one attempt at a solution—though an unsatisfactory one.

---

1. The accompanying diagram shows the formation of Macdonald' s corps at Wagram. This formation has always been criticized on the assumption that it was intended to break the enemy's line by sheer weight. My impression is that no such idea entered Macdonald's head, he was far too experienced a man to have made such an error; rather, it would appear to me, it was deliberately adopted on the assumption that the big battery of 100 guns which preceded it would so far shatter the enemy's fire power that it would experience but little resistance in the actual passage of the enemy's position, but would then encounter the furious attacks of his reserves, in front and

Generally the battle developed in accordance with the spirit which underlay the strategy. The object of the opening attacks was *to hold,* not merely to *see.* To meet them the enemy was compelled to bring up his reserves, and then began a struggle of will-power between the opposing leaders, in which Napoleon invariably won, because of his innate gift of command. *For the time being he ceased to be open to the play of human sympathy.* His best regiments might die in ranks as they stood, his most trusted leaders, seeing themselves on the point of annihilation, might clamour for reinforcements, but nothing touched him *until the moment came when his instinct told him that the "battle was ripe"* as he expressed it, and the psychic force (which really wins battles) was waning faster in his opponents' ranks than in his own. Then the last reserves were brought forward, every available battery dashed to the front, and at case shot ranges blew a hole in the enemy's battle line, through which the Cavalry and Infantry could penetrate. This idea was a century old. It is to

on the flanks, to meet which it would be essential to have the whole corps in hand ready to fight in any direction.

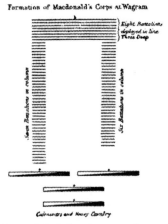

Formation of Macdonald's Corps at Wagram

Be this as it may, as a fact it failed, for the men threw themselves down and allowed themselves to be trampled on. There is a tradition in the French Army, cited by Armand du Pic, that only 3,000 reached the enemy's position and about 3,000 were killed; therefore the remaining 24,000 obviously did not go on.

be found in Guibert, du Teil and other writers, and is based on the analogy of the breach in a fortress, *but not until the association of the Artillery with the Infantry in permanent Divisions* had been carried into effect was it possible to overcome the technical difficulties in its execution. It was not really until the battle of Friedland, in 1807, that the machinery at last overcame its own internal resistance.

Indirectly this use of Napoleon's Artillery solved the problem of utilizing his very inefficient Cavalry on the battlefield. In Frederick's day, it was normally impossible to decide beforehand at what point the services of the Cavalry would be needed, hence a high degree of manoeuvring capacity was necessary to ensure its arrival at the right time and place. Now it became possible to predict with certainty where it would be required a considerable time in advance, and to move it into position without excessive demands on pace or manoeuvring powers. Once formed it could be let loose to ride down its opponents by sheer weight of numbers, like the Rhattor horse against du Boigne's brigades at the battle of Jeypore.[1]

The Cavalry of the Allies throughout 1813 was generally of a far higher standard than that of the French, but as its Leaders could not determine where it was likely to be required, much greater demands on its endurance and drill efficiency were necessarily made, which it was not always in a position to satisfy. With the assured sense of superiority resulting from his possession of a strategic system and a tactical proficiency superior to anything his adversaries could

---

1. Charge of the Rhattor Horse. *Note:* The description of this charge in Skinner's *Memoire* is unfortunately too long to quote Briefly, 10,000 Rhattor Horse, formed in a huge column, attacked the regular Mahratta Infantry under du Boigné, who stood in squares to meet them. They reserved their fire till the horsemen were almost on them, but it hardly checked the momentum of the charge. The mass swept over the squares like a tidal wave, and of 8,000 Infantry only 200 are said to have escaped. See *Cavalry versus Infantry,* p. 167, by the Author.

oppose to him, *Napoleon now tended towards over-confidence, and sometimes discounted his victory in advance, with consequences which ultimately became fatal both to his Army and himself.* This tendency must be kept in mind as a basis of all criticism of the coming Campaign.

CHAPTER 3

The Prologue of the War

It was on December 4, 1812, that Napoleon left the wreck of the Grand Army, which six months ago he had led across the Niemen, to its fate in the snows of Russia. Handing the command of this pitiful remnant over to Murat, he hurried back to Paris as fast as post horses could carry him. On the 14th he was in Dresden. From there he wrote to the King of Prussia, calling on him to raise another 30,000 men,[1] an order with which the King was most willing to comply, as it afforded cover under which to continue preparations for the national emergency which all Germans felt must arise sooner or later. On December 19 Napoleon arrived in Paris and wrote to Murat a letter,[2] in which he made it appear that the King of Prussia had himself offered these reinforcements. No evidence of any such offer has, however, been found, and the motive which led to this distortion of fact remains obscure, unless Napoleon craftily intended to put fresh heart into his beaten and famishing soldiers by leading them to believe that the Prussians still had a good enough opinion of their invincibility to offer to back them up in spite of their retreat from Moscow.

On January 19, 1813, the Emperor wrote to Davoût, then in Hamburg,[3] ordering him to seize Swedish Pomerania

1. *Corres.* 19,385.
2. *Corres.* 19,388.
3. *Correa.* 16,447.

forthwith, if there were boots enough in store there to make it worth his while. The order was promptly carried out, but the boots had to be dearly paid for, as this violation of Swedish territory was not the least of the causes which subsequently compelled Bernadotte to throw in his lot with the Allies.

Meanwhile, the débris of Napoleon's beaten army was reaching the Prussian frontier, and a report of the Q.M.G. of Königsberg shows that on December 21 there were 255 French generals, 699 colonels, 4,412 captains and subalterns, and 26,590 men, exclusive of 6,000 sick in the hospital, quartered in that district alone.

As the stragglers arrived at the frontier they were ordered to report at the following places:—

I and VIII Corps at Thorn; II and III at Marienburg; IV and IX at Marienwerder; V at Warsaw; VI at Plock; Artillery and Engineers at Danzig; Dismounted Line Cavalry at Königsberg; Guard Cavalry at Elbing.

The 30th Division (Heudelet) consisting of Bavarians, together with 8 Squadrons, had only recently reached Danzig, and were the only formed body of troops available for the field.

The X Corps, (Macdonald), to which the Prussian contingent under Yorck was attached, was still in the neighbourhood of Riga, and the VII Corps (Reynier) was with Schwarzenberg close to the Austrian frontier. The Russians had halted about Vilna, and on the Bug, only following up the French retreat with their Cossacks, who on December 21 crossed the Prussian frontier near Gumbinen and Insterburg. On December 30, the convention of Tauroggen was concluded, by which von Yorck separated himself from Macdonald and surrendered to the Russians. The exact truth of this surrender will probably never be ascertained, for many verbal messages passed between Yorck and the King in Berlin, of which under the circumstances no written record exists. The situation was far too delicate to entrust such secrets to paper.

General von Wrangel, in his *Memoirs,* published in 1830, says that in August, 1812, he carried verbal instructions to von Grawert, authorizing him, in case of a general retreat, to separate from the French and withdraw on Graudenz, but von Grawert had just resigned his command on account of sickness, and the message was delivered to his successor, von Yorck, who, however, did not show himself at all inclined to act upon verbal instructions in a matter of such moment. But already at an early stage of the proceedings a kind of tacit agreement had been arrived at to limit the fighting at the outposts "as far as was compatible with the honour of the Prussian arms," which was also a portion of the verbal instructions conveyed by von Wrangel, then a Major and confidential Staff Officer. The Russians kept Yorck well informed as to the progress of the retreat, and from time to time made efforts to induce him to desert the French cause, but to all these Yorck returned answer that he had been all his life a soldier, knew nothing of diplomacy, and must carry out his orders. At length, in December, the collapse of the French Army becoming more evident every day, Yorck transmitted a fresh proposal of the Russians to Berlin for the Royal instructions, and a Major von Seydlitz was sent to him again with verbal instructions, the precise import of which cannot be discovered, for the testimony of the eye-witnesses of the several interviews which now took place differs on several essential points. All that seems certain is that von Seydlitz's verbal message actually did authorize Yorck to act "according to circumstances," and these presently became so pressing, with the prospect of becoming immediately worse, that on the night of December 29 Yorck agreed to a meeting for the next day, at which the final terms of surrender were agreed upon with the Russians.

The King received the news of this surrender with every symptom of the gravest disapproval, and played his part so well that all the Court were convinced that his anger was most real. But a letter of the late Emperor William I, dated

May 15,1869[1] gives a somewhat different complexion to the matter. The news had been brought to the King at Potsdam, who with the old Emperor William, then a boy of about sixteen, and other members of his family, was walking in the grounds of San Souci. The King went away to speak with the messenger, Graf. Henckel von Donnersmarck, and—

> .... for about half an hour we waited in extreme anxiety. Then the King returned with an expression of satisfaction on his face which we had not seen for a long time, but which seemed quite out of harmony with the little speech he made to the assembled group, amongst whom were our respective adjutants and governors. 'Graf. Henckel has brought me bad news. Yorck has capitulated with his corps to the Russians; the times of 1806 seem about to repeat themselves.'

The Nation, of course, received the news with the warmest satisfaction, and when, as its immediate consequence, the French were found to be resuming their retreat, this satisfaction broke out into enthusiasm, which proved seriously embarrassing to the King, to whose insight into the situation and strength of character history has never rendered the justice which they deserve.

Few men have ever- been placed in a more difficult position. Because at the crisis of Jena, being then a young and inexperienced man, he had not overridden the opinions of the war-seasoned Generals, by whom he was surrounded, he has been credited with a weakness of purpose and want of capacity very much in excess of his deserts.

No unprejudiced man can read, either his comments on the many reform projects submitted to him before the catastrophe, or the regulations for which he was personally responsible, without being struck by the clear, practical common-sense

---

1. *Holleben*, p. 86.

brought to bear upon every subject. This quality of his always grasped the whole of a matter where his relatively irresponsible advisers saw only their own part in it. After the War he had to conquer the confidence of his Army and his people over again. To do so, in the interests of the Nation, he played a part moat repugnant to his strictly honourable nature, which revolted at the duplicity required by the urgency of the situation.

From the very first it is abundantly clear that he meant to prepare Prussia for the re-conquest of her political independence, but as events have abundantly proved, he knew the temper of his people and the amazing power of Napoleon far more thoroughly than did the reformers. He knew quite well that the French Emperor would never rest without an effort to retrieve his fame; such an effort was indeed a prime necessity of his continued existence, and the King of Prussia not only gauged the yet untouched resources of the French Empire with rare accuracy, but he divined, and rightly, as events were soon to prove, the want as yet of any real depth of national patriotism in his own people. The reforms of Stein and Hardenberg were the corner-stone of real military efficiency, and these needed nearly two generations of activity before the spirit of parochialism, the characteristic of the period, could be welded into a coherent and imperial whole.[1]

All doubts as to the military importance of Yorck's action are set at rest by Napoleon's own opinion. On January 19 he wrote to Jerome in the following words (*Corres.* 19,462):

> The immediate consequences of this act of treachery are that the King of Naples will have to withdraw behind the Vistula, and that my losses will be increased by all the sick left in the hospitals of Old Prussia.

---

1. The population of Prussia being 4,800,000, there should have been not less than 420,000 men still of an age to bear arms, of which less than 100,000 were actually with the colours; yet only 10,000 responded to the call for volunteers between January 1 and June 31. Evidently the spirit of the time was hardly ripe for Scharnhorst's reforms.

Clausewitz, who was present with Wittgenstein's Head-quarters, confirmed this by his independent testimony to the effect that the Russian Army was so completely exhausted by its losses that had Yorck and Macdonald remained together, the pursuit must have come to a standstill on the Niemen, and all the resources of East Prussia would have been paralysed for months to come. As it was, East Prussia proved the nucleus of the Nation's revival, for the Cossacks pressing on the heels of the French gave the necessary screen behind which the first new formations could be organized, without news of them reaching the French Emperor.

The situation was indeed one that called for all the King of Prussia's perspicacity. At Berlin he was still within the clutches of his adversary, and might at any moment be taken prisoner. To avoid this risk he left Berlin on January 22, and betook himself to Breslau.

On his way he wrote to Napoleon, pointing out in diplomatic language that though he was most anxious to fulfil his treaty obligations, money was an indispensable condition of his compliance, and that if the French Government's payment for the supplies issued to French troops during the previous year was forthcoming (as provided for in their agreement) the process of rearmament would be greatly facilitated.[1]

Meanwhile, the Estates of East Prussia met on their own initiative at Königsberg, being cut off from direct communication with their King, who officially, was still the Ally of Napoleon, by the Russian screen of Cossacks, and with great enthusiasm passed a resolution in favour of placing all the resources of the district at the disposal of Yorck, Bülow and Borstell, the principal military representatives on the spot, and they proceeded to call out the quotas of men due under the existing law from the several parishes. But though the towns-people were ready to welcome all signs of military activity,

---

1. The amount claimed was 100 million francs.

the peasants in the country showed no corresponding zeal for the National Cause. The orders directing the recruits to join their headquarters were torn up, the civil authorities were openly defied, and ultimately dragoons had to be sent round the provinces to enforce obedience to the law.[1]

Arrived at Breslau, Frederick William came more within the direct influence of the Russians, and on February 23 decided openly to throw in his lot with theirs; but his celebrated proclamation denouncing the French Alliance, and calling on the whole Nation to rise against their oppressors, was only published on March 16, and the actual declaration of War did not reach Paris until the 27th of the same month.

Looking at the numbers actually brought into the field by the date of the first great battle of the War of Liberation, Lützen or Gross Gorschen, on May 2, *viz*. 95,000 Allies against 145,000 French, one is inclined to think that an even longer delay could only have been advantageous, for the great difficulties in raising fresh troops consisted in laying the foundations of a sound organization and system of administration, matters not easily attended to when once active contact with the enemy has been established. Once it is quite clear who is really responsible for clothing and equipment, who is authorized to sign requisitions and decree new formations, etc., fresh units are comparatively easily called into existence. But all such machinery was idle in the districts still held by the French or occupied by the Russians, who were still technically the enemy; while the poverty of the country, its comparative roadlessness, and more particularly the alternations of frost and thaw, made the circulation of orders and instructions most tedious and unreliable.

To overcome, as far as possible these difficulties, the King decided on a bold step, i.e. decentralization. Accordingly he decreed on March 15 the sub-division of the King-

---

1. See *V.* Holleben.

dom into four Military Governments, viz., *(a)* the district between the Elbe and Oder, General von L'Estocq; *(b)* between the Oder and Vistula, Lieut. General von Tauentzien; (c) between the Vistula and Russian frontier, Lieut.-General von Massenbach, and *(d)* the district of Silesia, Lieut.-General Graf. Götzen—within each of which divisions the civil authorities were made responsible for the supply of recruits, equipment, etc., while the military authorities undertook the organization of the men thus supplied, their training, and all matters of local defence. Each unit as it was formed and completed was at once drafted to the Field Army. It will be clear that even a couple of weeks' delay would have been invaluable to allow this new machinery to work smoothly; but at the last, events forced the hands of the King. Napoleon's demands for the supply of fresh troops, and his claim to place Prussian commands at the disposal of his Marshals for employment against the "common enemy" became too insistent, while on the other hand the continuous advance of the Cossacks, who drove the French out of Berlin on March 3 and 4, 1813, rendered further delay impossible.

Reading and re-reading the mass of documentary evidence accumulated by von Holleben, from whom the above figures and facts are principally taken, an unbiased critic is absolutely forced to the conclusion that the King showed sounder judgment than all his advisers put together, although their list comprises such names as Scharnhorst, Bülow, Blücher, Hardenberg and Stein; their ideas were premature, his were practical.

On March 15 Scharnhorst submitted to the King a final project for the organization of a *Landwehr* and *Landsturm* throughout the whole kingdom, which was finally approved on the 17th of the same month. The project had indeed been under discussion for months, and the fundamental idea, together with the name, can be traced back to 1658; but the poverty of the country was so great, and the different degrees in which districts were or had been affected by the passage through them of French or Russian troops, prevalence of active hostilities, and so forth, had hitherto rendered any attempt to deal with the matter on a uniform basis, if not impossible, at any rate inopportune. Even as it was, such delays arose in its execution that no formed bodies of Landwehr actually took part in field operations until after the Armistice of June 4, though isolated detachments, temporarily called together without uniforms or even muskets, rendered good service in support of the field troops, both in liages, and in the operations on the Lower Elbe before Napoleon's reappearance on the scene in the beginning of May. Permission was also given by the King of Prussia to form Volunteer Corps, and though these too were not employed until after the Armistice, a recapitulation of their names here will be in place. These volunteers found their own equipment, and were commanded by ex-regular officers.

They were "The Lützow Free Corps," whose formation, sanctioned on February 18, reached on March 21 a strength of 1,036 men, organized in 4 Companies, and 2 Squadrons, to which subsequently a Battery of 3 guns and 1 howitzer were added.

The foreign battalion, "von Reusz," and the volunteer rifles, "von Reiche,"[1] both formed of volunteers drawn from the rest of Germany, and nearly all deserters from the Westphalian or other contingents of the "Grand Army."

Major Hellwig's volunteers, 2 Squadrons of partisan Cavalry; Major von Schifl's Hussar detachment—commanded by a brother of the celebrated von Schill, killed in a raid near Stralsund, 1809—comprised 2 Squadrons. Also a variety of smaller detachments, mostly composed of picked foresters, even of poachers amnestied.

---

1. "Von Reusz" and "von Reiche" were the names of their Commanders, not standing, as the names would suggest, in any connexion with the little kingdom of Reusz or the Empire.

The total of all these formations up to the date of the Armistice only reached the figure of 8,500 men, of whom 2,000 were mounted.[1]

By the end of March there stood ready for the field—

(a) 21 Battalions, 40 Squadrons, 12½ Batteries, 2 companies' engineers = 646 officers, 26,510 men, 100 guns—under Blücher.

(b) 27 Battalions, 24 Squadrons, 11½ Batteries, 4 Companies' engineers = 646 officers, 25,751 men, 106 guns—under Yorck and Bülow.

(b) 4 Battalions, 4 Squadrons, 1½ Batteries = 61 officers, 2,761 men, 12 guns—under Borstell.

Other small detachments brought the numbers up to 57 Battalions, 70 Squadrons, 27½ Batteries, 7 Companies engineers, 8 park columns, and 1 column tradesmen—in all 1,145 officers, 58,865 men, 234 guns available for field service, but their sick list was very high. In addition there remained 30,077 garrison troops, and 33,640 in the depots, giving a grand total of 122,582 men.

Compared with the states for August 1, 1811, these figures show a net increase of 48,169 men, which, even allowing for losses in Russia and a high rate of sickness, seem very small for such an emergency, and appears insignificant compared with the recreation of the French Army during the same period.

---

1. As an indication of the difficulties encountered in raising fresh bodies of troops, the case of Colonel von Thuimen's detachment may be cited.
Von Thuimon equipped 8J Battalions in forty-eight hours, and then started on a march of 150 miles through country held by the French. To avoid observation, he had frequently to march by night The inhabitants proved very lukewarm to the cause, many of the men deserted, and more broke down through hardships entailed by want of clothing, shelter and food.
The origin of the black uniforms of Lütow's Volunteers had nothing to do with the "death or glory" sentiment, but was adopted as the simplest means of making use of the black civilian coats which the men normally wore, and of the stores of cloth in the tailors' shop. Both cloth and tailors had frequently to be requisitioned.—See *Von Holleben,* Vol. I.

It cannot be doubted that the Prussians as a race were far more alive to the necessity for personal service than were the French, who had not felt the burden of invasion for twenty years, and then only very partially, about one-eighth of the total area of that country only having been affected. The chief difference would seem to be that in France civil and military Government had been accustomed to work together for a whole generation, while for nearly two generations in Prussia military Government had been entirely subordinate to the civilians, and the Army and Nation had drifted completely out of touch with each other.

It is interesting also to compare the relative yield of fresh armed men in England in 1803 under *threat* of invasion only. In that year we raised nearly 600,000 fighting men on a population about three times greater than that of Prussia, the influx, of course, being greatest during the first six months after the King's message of the 5th March announcing the renewal of hostilities after the Peace of Amiens, and our sick list of course was much less. Yet, making all due allowances, it would seem that our output per cent, was at least double that of the Prussians.[1]

The most amazing point, however, seems to me to be this, in spite of all the efforts of the Tugendbund and other secret societies, to say nothing of the inspiring *Volkslieder* of Arndt, etc., the two weak battalions of Reusz and Reiche appear to have been quite adequate to absorb all the true patriots of the remaining 20 million Germans.

Considerable difficulty was also experienced in finding new officers for the Forces. The conditions of the entrance examinations had to be relaxed, and the two cadet schools were suppressed, their pupils being posted direct to Regiments. Non-commissioned officers of good character and ap-

---

1. The comparison between the realized military output of France in 1792 is also interesting. See Max Jahns, *Das Französiche Herr.*

proved conduct in the field were also freely promoted. The cause of the difficulty, of course, lay in the Treasury policy of the past forty years, which had compelled the retention of officers on the active list long after they ought to have been pensioned. It was not that the Generals of the pre-Jena Army had been too old, but the captains and senior subalterns decidedly were so (the former averaged about the same as those who served under Moltke in the Franco-German War, and were younger than the average of French Generals ten years ago); they had lost all youth and activity, and collapsed wholesale under the stress of the retreat.

As regards muskets, there appear to have been sufficient for the Field Army, but the depot and garrison troops had to drill with extemporized pikes, while some of the *Landwehr*, even after the Armistice, were led against the enemy their front ranks provided only with similar weapons. The supply of guns, too, was sufficient, though heavy and antiquated patterns had to be employed,[1] and both the draught horses and cavalry remounts appear to have been fair material, though time was wanted to train them in the systematic manner of former days, and, as Marwitz[2] and others have since shown us, this training was the real secret of excellence in the old Frederickian Cavalry.

English subsidies were largely instrumental in rendering

---

1. It must not be forgotten that the last fifty years had seen an enormous progress in artillery construction, almost as great as the step from the ordinary B.L. guns of the nineties to the present quick firers. The guns had been rendered immensely more powerful in proportion to the weight behind the trains, while the method of draught and finish of the carriage had also undergone great improvement. Gribeauval in France, and Scharnhorst in Hanover and Prussia had been principally instrumental in securing these reforms. (See M. Colin's *Education de Napoleon.*)
2. Marwitz's book is now very difficult to obtain and was never translated. Prince Hohenlohe von Ingelfingen's *Conversations on Cavalry* gives the best information on this subject. I may also refer to my own *Cavalry, its Past and Future,* which gives useful details on both the French and German cavalry at this period.

the equipment of these troops possible. Unfortunately, we also sent over a number of uniforms of English pattern (colour not stated), and, to quote Von Holleben, "The King had to submit to the daily annoyance of seeing his men clad in these tasteless garments." Actually this insult seems to rankle in that author's mind even more than all the exactions of the French Marshals, whose characters he now seeks to whitewash at the expense of his ancestors' reputation for veracity in the past. However, before long the King had his revenge, for shortly after Waterloo the Prussian cap and frock coat was adopted wholesale in the British Army, and at the present moment it would be impossible to distinguish between Prussian and British troops on a misty morning at fifty yards range.

Meanwhile the Russian Field Army had been moving forward, leaving detachments

behind to observe the fortresses of Thorn, Danzig and Küstrin—in all 36,000 men, 313 guns; and troops to keep order in Poland—21,800 men, 150 guns. Making these deductions, however, at the end of March, 1813, the troops available for the Field Army numbered 63,686 men and 436 guns,[1] of whom 19,000 with 92 guns under Wittgenstein constituted an Advance Guard that was pressing close on the heels of the retiring French, while the remainder under Kutusow were drawing near to Kalisch on the borders of Silesia.

It is time now to return to the operations of the wreck of the Grand Army, which, as we have seen above, had been compelled to evacuate in haste the banks of the Vistula on receipt of the news of Yorck's defection at Tauroggen. Murat's orders we have already given; these were the last he issued, as he was immediately afterwards recalled to Paris, and handed over his command to Prince Eugène, Viceroy of Italy. At this moment, January 19, the whole of the six Corps, nominally at the Prince's disposal gave him barely 12,000 fighting men,

---

1. *Bdleben,* p. 266.

and these almost worn out by privation. He would have had practically no men for field operations, but for the arrival at Posen of some 10,000 provisional detachments of different nationalities; for the only other troops which had preserved their formation, *viz.*, the Polish Division, Grand Jean, of Macdonald's Corps, and Heudelet's Division of the XI Corps had been thrown into Danzig, raising the garrison of that place to 30,000 men, of whom, however, barely two-thirds were fit for active service.

On the right wing the VII Corps (Reynier), two Saxon Divisions and the French Division (Durutte) had separated themselves from Schwarzenberg's command when the latter concluded an armistice with the Russians, and were marching through Silesia, suffering continually from the attacks of Cossacks and other local partisans. But Poniatowski's Poles, about 8,000 men, had been cut off in Warsaw, and another 12,000 had been left as garrisons in Modlin, Zamosc and Thorn. In rear of the centre there remained only the 31st Division (Lagrange) of the XI Corps, 10,000 strong, but dispersed to hold Berlin and garrison Magdeburg Spandau and the fortresses on the Oder—Glogau, Küstrin and Stettin, whilst the Division of Grenier, 18,000 men, was only due in Berlin on January 25.

Out of the 12,000 men thus immediately under Prince Eugene's hand he organized four weak Divisions—one Bavarian (General Rechberg), one Polish (General Girard), one French (General Gérard), and finally one of the Guard (General Roguet), grouping them around Posen, and drafting all supernumerary officers and non-commissioned officers in excess of their complements back to the depot at Erfurt. The name "Division" was retained in order to deceive the enemy as to their actual weakness. Some 2,000 mounted men, partly surplus to the above detachments, partly rallied to him by force of circumstances, were also organized in two "Divisions." With this skeleton force the Prince endeavoured to impose on the Russians and hold the line of the Oder in obedience to the Emperor's orders, until reinforcements from France could reach him. He also summoned Bülow and all other Prussian detachments to his aid, but received evasive answers. Meanwhile the growing unrest in Berlin and its neighbourhood compelled him to keep back the new XI Corps, organized out of Grenier's 18,000 men, for the maintenance of order in his rear.

His situation soon became hopelessly untenable. Frost held all the rivers in its bonds, and Tettenborn's and Tschitschagow's Cossacks swept all round his flanks. At length on February 12 he began his retreat, reaching Frankfort on the Oder on February 18, where hearing that the Cossacks had already crossed the river further to the north, he continued his movement on Berlin. Meanwhile in the south Reynier's two Saxon Divisions deserted him, and Durutte's Division was surprised on the march and nearly cut to pieces.

But even Berlin (where he had rallied on the new XI Corps, to which Gouvion St. Cyr had been appointed in command,) could not, as we have seen, be held for long, and on March 5 the Viceroy's (Prince Eugene's) force withdrew to the Elbe, whilst the wreck of Reynier's troops gathered in Dresden. Napoleon wrote one of his characteristic letters to Eugène, censuring him severely, but more as an elder brother than as a *Generalissimo*, for his failure to hold the line of the Oder; but his reasoning, though unanswerable from the armchair-critical standpoint, like his letters to Jerome when in Spain, made no sufficient allowance for circumstances of weather and topography.

If the old school of strategists had gone altogether too far in the attention they paid to the configuration of the ground and other circumstances which exist only to be conquered by skill and determination, he now overshot the limit of the reasonable in ignoring the limits of human endurance and climatic vicissitudes. To him as Graf. Yorck von Wartenburg in his *Napoleon as a General* has well pointed out, a "Corps" remained always a "Corps," even if its numbers had shrunk to 5,000 men or less, while a river or a mountain range was a scratch on a map, unless he happened at the moment to be face to face with it himself. In this instance he had entirely overlooked the terrible frost which still held all the rivers of Eastern Prussia in its grip. Had the Oder been in its normal unfordable condition, undoubtedly the possession of its four fortresses, Stettin, Frankfort, Küstrin and Glogau, might have enabled Eugène to hold it, even with his reduced forces for some weeks longer than he actually did, as the Russian Army was still a long way off and Yorck and Büllow's forces were quite insignificant. But in the weather then prevailing the Oder could be crossed almost anywhere, as, in fact, it was, and with a population on the verge of insurgence behind him, the Viceroy certainly had not a moment to spare when he came to his decision to retreat.

On the question of the abandonment of Berlin, Napoleon's comments are again masterly from the *general* point of view, although, as above pointed out, no allowance is made for the actual position of affairs as seen by the average man on the spot.

Nothing is less in accord with sound Military practice than your decision to withdraw your Headquarters behind Berlin (*viz.*, to Schöneberg, a preliminary step to complete withdrawal). It should have been evident to you that this step must attract the enemy. If, on the contrary, you had taken up a position in front of Berlin (i.e. east) communicating by convoys with Spandau, and thence with Magdeburg, and had brought up a Division of the V Corps (from Magdeburg) midway between the two latter points, and had constructed there a few redoubts, the enemy would have believed that you intended to offer battle. Hence he would not have passed the Oder until he had united 60,000 to 80,000 men, which he was far from being in a condition to do.

As a fact, on March 4 the Russians were still five days'
march from Berlin, Yorck and Bülow even further; but there
is no evidence to show that the Viceroy was aware of this,
and in view of the hopeless inadequacy of his mounted
forces and the nature of the country, it seems hardly possible
that he could have scouted efficiently to that end. Napoleon
then continues:

> The day on which your Headquarters retired behind
> Berlin you practically advertised your determination
> not to hold that town, and thus lost that attitude of
> determined opposition which it is the real Art of War
> to know how to keep. An experienced General in your
> place would have established a camp (presumably en-
> trenched) in front of (i.e. east of) Küstrin, and thus have
> gained time to draw forward the Corps on the Elbe to
> Berlin. He could not then have been attacked except at
> the cost of the time it would have taken the enemy to
> prepare the wide sweeping movements the capture of
> such a position would have entailed.[1]

Eugène, however, seems to have had but little choice in the
matter of his retreat, and appears to have considered even the
Magdeburg road, to which the Emperor refers, as not safe enough
for his retrograde movement, for, in fact, he retreated in two columns, the principal one on Wittenberg, the other by Lückau on
Torgau, a Saxon fortress still held by Saxon troops, who declined
to allow the French to pass on the grounds that Saxony was a
neutral country. Refused passage here, the column bent off up
stream to Meissen, where it arrived most conveniently in time to
assist Reynier in overawing the people of Dresden.

---

1. References to this maintenance of "an attitude of determined opposition,"
are frequent in Napoleon's comments and criticisms, and their plain com-
monsense is perhaps the reason why they have been so frequently overlooked
by his commentators, who were too intent on discovering allusions to the
re-entering frontiers, angular relations of Unes of operations to bases, etc., to
have any attention to spare for the apparently obvious.

These movements brought the French troops into position along the Elbe, a cordon position of the worst kind; and here for the moment the Viceroy left them, till, his report having reached the Emperor, a storm of reproaches burst upon his head.

I do not see what obliged you to quit Berlin. Your movements are so rapid that you have not been able to take the direction I had prescribed[1].You have uncovered Magdeburg without having taken steps to assure yourself whether it is sufficiently provisioned or garrisoned[2]. Yet it contains all our Field Artillery, and many other important things.

By your march on Wittenberg you have left unprotected the whole of the 32nd 'Division Militaire' and the Kingdom of Westphalia.You thus run the risk of losing all the Cavalry which is distributed in cantonments, and have left the finest provinces of the Empire at the mercy of an advance guard of a few thousand men. I have always told you that you should retire on Magdeburg. In laying your lines of communication *via* Mayence, not only have you compromised the safety of the 32nd 'Division Militaire,' but also Holland and my squadrons in the Scheldt. It is really time to begin making war seriously. It is in front of Magdeburg (*i.e.* to the east of it) that you should have united 80,000 men, whence as a centre you would protect the whole of the Elbe. Our operations make us ridiculous in the eyes of our allies and of our enemies, because you constantly retreat a week before their infantry come within sight of you. It is really time that you should set to work and begin to operate like a soldier. I have laid down what you ought to do.

1.Alluding to a previous letter received too late for compliance with its mandates
2. This is hardly fair, as Eugène had, in fact, left there the whole V Corps, some 30,000 men.

Then follows in detail the plan the Emperor wishes to see carried out:

Prince Eugène takes position nine to twelve miles east of Magdeburg with the V and XI Corps, Roguet's Division, and the greater part of the Cavalry—65,000-70,000 men of the best available—and covers his camp with redoubts, leaving ample space to manœuvre between them. Marshal Victor with the 4th Division (12 Battalions) moves on the left bank of the Elbe to near Dessau, where he establishes a bridge, and till this is complete a ferry, covered by fortifications. His action will extend as far as Torgau, and the garrison of Wittenberg, raised to 2,000 men. General Reynier, with the 7th Corps[1] will ensure the watch over the line of the Elbe from Torgau to the mountains of Bohemia (about 70 miles); he will fortify the bridge at Meissen, The Saxon General commanding in Torgau will employ two-thirds of his force (4,000 men) to watch the river above and below the town; the rest will remain always in the place[2].

Marshal Davoût, with the 1st Division (16 Battalions) will place himself on the left of Magdeburg (i.e. north). He knows Hamburg and is known there too, and his proximity to that town will be very useful. Hamburg will have a garrison of 8,000 men, sufficient, with the aid of its municipal guards, to hold the town against the Cossacks. The King of Westphalia will organize a mixed Division of his troops, to be concentrated two or three marches west of Magdeburg, which will be ready to support either Victor or Davoût as the case may require.

Of course all the boats on the Elbe and its affluents on the right bank must be systematically destroyed, or

1. Which the Emperor imagined to be 12,000 strong, but which was in reality only 6,000.
2. As we have seen, the Saxon General refused to accept any orders from the French.)

brought under the protection of our own guns. The line of communications will be from Magdeburg on Wesel.

The principal Corps, placed in the camp in front of Magdeburg, will send out every day mixed reconnaissances of 1,500 horsemen and a Division of Infantry. I presume that you do not intend to let yourself be shut in by the Cossacks and a few Battalions.

In case of an attack directed against the principal Corps, Marshals Victor and Davoût will cross the river and manœuvre against the enemy's flanks.

Your position in the camp in front of Magdeburg will re-establish the 'moral' of your troops. If the enemy marches in force on Havelberg, he must leave at least 80,000 to mask you (and this is impossible, as the Allies have not a sufficient number of men available). If they make a serious effort towards Dresden, more than Reynier can deal with; then the latter will fall back behind the Mulde, or, further, always keeping on your right. Then an advance of the principal corps from Magdeburg or Brandenburg will frighten them and bring them back to the right bank of the Elbe again. In taking up this offensive position and showing the great number of troops you have in Magdeburg, the enemy will be held in check and will be unable to undertake anything without bringing at least 100,000 men against you; and seeing himself on the eve of a battle, he will take good care not to make any detachments which would weaken him.[1]

Although throughout this letter Napoleon had systematically overestimated Eugene's forces and underestimated those of the Allies, the form of defence is perfect; but before this letter reached its destination the Viceroy had made further dispositions which aggravated the evils of the first. He had

---

1. *Letter* of March 19. See also *Lanresac*, p. 65, *et seq.*

brought Davoût from Hamburg and sent him to command all the troops about Dresden, and had written to justify his previous measures. This brought down on him renewed reproaches, for, as Napoleon very rightly points out, "for General Reynier to withdraw from Dresden means nothing, but for a Corps (however weak) under the Prince of Eckmuhl to be compelled to retreat is quite another matter; it would show that we intended to defend that place, but did not dare to act up to our intention."

Ultimately on March 18, under renewed pressure from Napoleon and the news of the occupation of Hamburg by Tettenborn's Cossacks, orders were issued to concentrate in the form indicated in the Emperor's orders, but with the important exception that the bulk of his troops were retained on the left bank of the river.

Meanwhile, the news from Hamburg which reached the Viceroy became alarming. A rumour was in circulation that 10,000 to 15,000 British troops were expected there, to form the nucleus of a Corps of 10,000 Danes, 5,000 Russians, and some thousand Swedes, their object being an attack on the 32nd Division Militaire and a descent thence on the Viceroy's communications with the Rhine. Napoleon was evidently much annoyed at the facility with which such rumours gained credence, and he administered to his unfortunate son-in-law the following reproof:

> You go altogether too quickly, and alarm yourself too readily. You attach too much importance to every rumour. More calm is required in the direction of military matters, and before attaching credence to reports they should be carefully discussed. Everything that spies and agents tell you (unless they have seen with their own eyes) is nothing, and even when they have seen, it is worth very little. Why do you believe that the British are going to disembark at Hamburg? Where are their

means? All their efforts are directed towards Portugal. Is it because a number of ships are in view? But you can see thousands every day from the coast of France. What I tell you is all useless, because it is only experience which teaches one to reduce these astonishing reports to their true dimensions.

Actually this censure was in excess of the Viceroy's deserts, for the Cossacks had spread far into the territory of the 32nd "Division Militaire," and as the inhabitants had risen in many places, it was almost impossible for any accurate idea of the enemy's movements to be ascertained.

On March 31, however, definite news was received to the effect that Wittgenstein had quitted Berlin on the 27th, and was marching on Rosslau to cross the Elbe at that place. The Prince now decided to bring his troops over the river to the position indicated in Napoleon's instructions in front of Magdeburg, and from this movement resulted a straggling encounter known as the Combat of Möckern on April 3, 4 and 5, only noticeable from the extreme fury with which the raw Prussian troops fought. Their numbers, however, were far less than Eugène had been led to expect, hence when by the evening of the 5th it had become apparent that there were not 20,000 men engaged in front of him, he concluded that the real main body of the enemy must still be on the march towards Rosslau with the intention of turning his right flank by the left bank of the river, and a report coming in stating that the bridge at Rosslau actually had been captured (a false rumour, as it afterwards turned out to be), he ordered his troops back to the left bank of the Elbe, and the Prussians were far too spent by their exertions to interfere with them.

The whole incident was unfortunate for the French, for the Allies made the most of their success, and the reports of it went far and wide all over Germany, raising confidence everywhere in the hearts of the patriotic party, which as yet was far from being synonymous with the whole Nation. Contrasting Eugene's action with Napoleon's orders, one can only ask oneself wonderingly, what possible cause there could have been strong enough to compel the Emperor to leave this most important command in such incapable hands, when all the time there was on the spot perhaps the ablest and most determined of all his Marshals: Davoût—a man of his own age—active and resolute far beyond the common standard, and devoted to Napoleon heart and soul. Every commentator in turn has asked this question, but hitherto no adequate reply has been suggested.

The Prince now recognizing the impossibility of continuing to hold the line of the Elbe determined to defend the Lower Saale, and during the following days the Army of the Elbe moved into position. Wittgenstein having now no enemy in front of him crossed the Elbe at Rosslau on the 10th, and moved southward to gain touch with Winzingerode and Blücher, whose cavalry scouts already watched the whole line of the Saale, and whose troops were disseminated between Leipzig and Dresden, whilst the Russian Main Army still lay at Kalisch, retained there by Kutusow in spite of the protestations of the Prussians. It was only on April 7 that the Russian Guards commenced their march on Dresden, distant 200 miles; hence they could not be expected to reach Leipzig, 90 miles further on, before the 27th or 28th of the month.

Till that date therefore the Allies had not more than 70,000 men available. Hence of necessity they called a halt and busied themselves in the improvement of communications, notably of bridges across the Elbe at Meissen and Dresden, whilst Wittgenstein attempted to surprise Wittenberg, but was repulsed.

On April 19 a rumour, premature as it turned out to be, that Napoleon was in full march at the head of the Army of the Maine to effect a junction with that of Prince Eugène, startled them into activity. Wittgenstein moved to Düben, Kleist to Halle, and Bülow, left before Magdeburg, was relieved by a small Russian corps of observation, and also rejoined the main body.

CHAPTER 4

The Battle of Lutzen

It is time now to return to the Emperor, and to review his activity during these months of heavy strain. The general idea governing the reconstruction of his Army has already been given in Chapter 2. Now it is necessary to build up the skeleton into which the raw material available was to be filled.

By a decree issued from the Trianon, March 12, the composition of the Army was laid down as follows—

I Corps	Marshal Davoût (Prince d'Eckmühl).	1st, 2nd and 3rd Divisions
II Corps	Marshal Victor (Duc de Belluno)	4th, 6th and 6th Divisions
III Corps	Marshal Ney (Prince de la Moskova)	the existing I Corps of Observation on the Rhine, together with the 8th, 9th, 10th and 11th Divisions
IV Corps	General Bertrand	the existing Corps of Observation in Italy, with the 12th, 13th, 14th and 15th Divisions
V Corps	General Lauriston	the existing Corps of Observation on the Elbe, with the 16th, 17th, 18th and 19th Divisions
VI Corps	Marshal Marmont (Duc de Ragusa),	the existing II Corps of Observation on the Rhine, with the 20th, 21st, 22nd, and 23rd Divisions

VII Corps	General Reynier	intended to comprise the two, Saxon Divisions, the 24th and 25th, and the 32nd Divisions (Durutte.)
VIII Corps	General Prince Poniatowski	Two Polish Divisions Nos. 26 and 27 (only partly raised)
IX Corps	No General named	The 28th and 29th Bavarian Divisions (never completed)
X Corps	General Rapp	in Danzig with the 7th, 30th and 33rd Divisions (old numbers), the remains of the old 34th Division were absorbed by the 30th
XI Corps	Marshal Gouvion St. Cyr	which had hitherto formed the Advance Guard on the Elbe, consisted of the 31st, 35th and 36th Divisions

Besides these troops, the Westphalians were to supply the 37th Division, the Würtembergers the 38th Division, the Hessians, Badeners, and Frankfurters the 40th Division, and ten Battalions organized in Erfurt were made into the 41st Division.

Subsequently on April 24, the formation of a XII Corps was decreed, and at a later date a XIII, Headquarters at Bamberg, was called into existence.

As a whole the plan was never realized, for, as already pointed out, circumstances proved even stronger than Napoleon's will, but as far as practicable each fresh unit organized was fitted into its appointed place, so that the framework of an Army existed from the very first, and the commands remained, whatever changes in detail might supervene. This was, of course, the fundamental idea in the much criticized paper Army Corps schemes for the British Army of the late Col. Home, R.E., revived by Mr. Brodrick; it is unfortunate that the true paternity of the idea was never put forward.

The procedure in individual cases may be studied with advantage.

The I Corps. The débris of the I Corps had rallied in Stettin, 68 officers, 1,536 non-commissioned officers and men, on February 17. An order of January 27 had originally laid down the strength of these Corps at four Divisions of 64 Battalions in all, of which the 1st Division was to be formed by 16 Battalions in Stettin itself, the 2nd Division (of another 16) in Erfurt, but on the evacuation of the Oder line this became impossible, and on February 10, the 1st Division began its formation in Leipzig. As the battalions (practically all new formations) only became ready in succession, and complete Divisions were required at the earliest possible date, all the 1st Battalions of Regiments went to the 1st Division, the 2nd Battalions to the 2nd Division, the 3rd and 4th Battalions in like manner to the 3rd and 4th Divisions, a method which was generally followed throughout the Army. The 1st and 2nd Divisions, commanded respectively by Phillipon and Dumonceau, were available for field service by the end of April.

The II Corps. Originally the Emperor had hoped to constitute this Corps out of the wreck of the old II and III Corps, but this proved quite impossible. No attempt, therefore, was made to build up the Battalions at the front. "But the Companies in the Oder fortresses will take the numbers of the Companies belonging to the 5th Battalions, and those of the 5th Battalions at the dépôts take the number of the Companies of the 1st Battalions, thus I shall have in France all the 1st Battalions at full strength"[1] as Napoleon wrote to his War Minister, General Clarke, on March 31, adding, "Each Regiment in the Grand Army will thus have four Battalions, with one or two Companies of the 5th Battalion in the Oder fortresses, and the balance of the 5th Battalion Companies will be at the dépôt."

Ultimately the 4th and 5th Divisions were formed at Magdeburg and Osnabrück respectively, and by the end of

---

1. *Corres.* 19,790.

April had attained the strength of—4th Division (Duberton), 12 Battalions, 8 guns, 7,000 men; 5th Division (Dufour), 11 Battalions, 8 guns, (5,979 men); and they were then moved up to the Elbe and Saale. The 6th Division did not reach the front till the end of June.

The III Corps. The original Corps of Observation on the Rhine, was built up of eight Regiments formed of the "Cohorts" of the old 22nd Regiment of the Line (4 Battalions), 10 provisional Regiments, and the 9th and 29th Light Infantry, both of two Battalions in all 60 Battalions. The Corps Headquarters were fixed at Mainz, and the Divisions were ordered to concentrate at Hanau, Frankfurt am Main, and Mainz. The 39th Division (Badeners, Hessians and Frankfurters) was also assigned to it as a 5th Division. Four Squadrons of the French 10th Hussars, and five Squadrons of the Baden Dragoons were further allotted to it, and by the end of April 44,764 men and 84 guns were available on the Saale. The Divisional Commanders were: 8th Division, Souham; 9th, Brenier; 10th, Girard; 11th Ricard; 39th, Marchand.

The IV Corps. Already on January 10, Napoleon notified the Italian chancellor (Melzi), of his intention to concentrate a Corps of Observation at Verona, and on February 27 informed him that the Corps must be ready on March 10 to set out for Augsburg. General Bertrand was to start with the first Division available, the others to follow as they were completed. Eight Battalions of "Cohorts", two Line Regiments with nine Battalions, 16 Battalions, conscripts of 1813, 13 Italian, one Algerian and three Neapolitan Battalions in all, were to supply the Infantry, and two Squadrons of Neapolitans, eight Squadrons of Würtembergers, the Cavalry. The Wurtemberg Division was also assigned to this Corps. Many delays arose in carrying out these orders, and only the 12th (Morand), and 15th (Peyri) Divisions, numbering 18,400 men with 37 guns, were available on the Saale by the end of April. The Würtembergers, 7,204 men, 12 guns, joined on the march, (May 4), at Freyburg (Saxony).

The V Corps. Eleven Regiments of "Cohorts" (44 Battalions), the 34th Regiment of the Line (four Battalions) and four foreign Battalions were assigned to this Corps, and the four Divisions, 16th, 17th, 18th, and 19th were at first ordered to be formed at Magdeburg, Münster, Osnabrück and Frankfurt am Main, but at the beginning of March they were all ordered up to Magdeburg, where Lauriston assumed the command. Towards the end of April they had attained a strength of 28,000 men (with 67 guns) unequally divided in the following manner—16th Division (Maison) eight Battalions, 17th(Puthod) 12 Battalions, 18th (Lagrange) 15 Battalions, 19th (Rochambeau) 12 Battalions, the 3rd Light Cavalry Brigade being assigned to them. The 17th (Puthod) was detached towards Hamburg and only rejoined on the battlefield of Bautzen, this left available at the end of April only 32 Battalions, 51 guns, in all 20,832 men.

The VI Corps. The II Corps of Observation on the Rhine became the VI Corps of the Grand Army, by the decree of March 12, and was to be collected about Mainz. The material available was 20 Battalions of Marines, eight provisional Line Battalions, four Battalions of the 37th Light Infantry, 10 other Light Infantry Battalions, and 16 Line Regiments.

The formation of this Corps met with all kinds of difficulties. Only fourteen Battalions of Marines had arrived on April 15. The 23rd Division (Teste) had only received two of its Battalions on the same date, and had to be left behind in Giessen and finally was only completed in Magdeburg in June, after the Armistice.

Thus only three Divisions, the 30th (Compans), 12 Battalions, 21st (Bouet) 13 Battalions, and 22nd (Friederichs) 14

Battalions, with 62 guns, making 24,250 men, were ready on the Saale at the end of April; only two Squadrons of Hessians had joined on May 1.

The VII Corps. The VII Corps had only the 32nd Division (Durutte) available, and on May 1 its strength amounted to only 102 officers, 903 men, with four guns.

The XI Corps. The XI Corps was principally constituted out of the only intact reinforcements for the Grand Army of 1812, on their way to the front in December of that year, *viz.* the 31st Division (Lagrange) of the old XI Corps, the very strong Division (Grenier), formed in November, 1812, in Verona, was divided into two Divisions on arrival at the front, which received the number 35 and 36. Seven Battalions of the 31st Division had been left behind in Stettin, and the remaining five were grouped with five others belonging to a temporary Division under Gerard, who received the command of the whole. Lagrange being recalled to France and given another command instead. Three Polish Battalions were also added, so that by the middle of March the Division, then at Meissen, numbered 13 Battalions, 12 guns. The 35th Division consisted of 12 Battalions and 22 guns, the 36th of 11 Battalions and 14 guns, but as the 31st Division was ordered to find 2,000 men for the garrison of Wittenberg, and to make other detachments, it was only six Battalions (about 3,000 strong) on the resumption of hostilities. The total strength of the Corps on April 15 was only 661 officers, 21,700 men. On April 22 General Gerard was again transferred to the 35th Division. General Ledhu received the 31st Division, and General Charpentier the 36th.

The XII Corps. The XII Corps was formed by a decree of April 24, by taking two Divisions, the 13th (Pacthod) and 14th (Lorencez), from the IV Corps and adding to it a Bavarian Division (Raglowich). The command of it was given to Oudinot (Duc de Reggio). On April 30 it was in the vicinity of Saalfeld 24,000 men and 50 guns strong.

We have already seen how the Viceroy had gathered a small body of the Old Guard under Roguet around him. On March 13 this little Division numbered 133 officers, 2,896 Infantry; 62 officers, 944 men. Cavalry, 4 officers and 188 men artillery and engineers.

About 1,000 other officers and non-commissioned officers for whom no men were available had been sent back by post to France, where on a nucleus supplied by 3,000 veterans of the Guard, who had volunteered to rejoin, they proceeded to reconstruct sixty Battalions of the Young Guard. Of these only one Division (Dumoustier), 16 Battalions and 52 guns, reached the front in time for the battle of Lützen, and a second (Delaborde) joined on May 25, at Dresden.

General Bessières received the command of the Cavalry of the Guard, which numbered 2,800 men, with two Horse Artillery batteries. It consisted of two Regiments of the Lancers, one of Chasseurs, one Dragoons, one Grenadiers, the celebrated Mameluke squadron, four Squadrons of *Elite Gendarmerie* and four Regiments of the *Gardes d'honneur* formed of young men of good family who had hitherto escaped the conscription by paying for substitutes, but at length had been caught by the same trick which was applied to the "Cohorts" The Cavalry of the whole Army was, as before mentioned, by far the weakest element of the whole force. It was organized in three Corps, of which the 1st had attained a strength of 172 officers, 3,343 men, 3,705 horses, on the Elbe and Saale, at the end of April. The 2nd, on April 15 numbered 149 officers, 3,144 men, and 3,581 horses; and the 3rd, which on May 1 was at Hanau, reported 3,895 men fit for duty.

Further formations were in progress throughout the whole of Europe at the time under the Napoleonic dominion, the details of which would require more space than it is possible to afford. However, the net outcome of the whole was that on May 1, 1813, the Emperor again stood at the head of 226,177 men, with 457 guns, which were subdivided into two Armies, the Army of the Main under his own command, and the Army of the Elbe under the Viceroy of Italy (Prince Eugène). To the former belonged the III, VI and IV Corps, the Guards on arrival, and the 3rd Cavalry Corps. The latter comprised the V and XI Corps and such portions of the I, II, and VII Corps as were available, together with the 1st and 2nd Cavalry Corps.

The above details will suffice to give some idea of the extraordinary results that can be accomplished with the most unpromising material, under most adverse circumstances, when there is a Man of iron will and resolute purpose at the head of affairs. If it is objected that Napoleons are few and far between, the answer is that this work of Army reorganization was only a portion of the whole task of Government which he accomplished, and that his plan bears evidence of haste and want of consideration at every turn, which presumably would not have occurred had he been free to give his whole mind to this one question. Moreover, the means of execution, i.e. telegraphs, telephones, railways, good maps, and most important of all, a Staff trained systematically to deal with these questions, are everywhere now available to aid the Leaders of to-day. Compared with what the Emperor actually accomplished in the four months between his arrival in Paris on December 19, and his departure for the front on April 14, any conceivable task that would fall to the lot of a British Commander-in-Chief, even the organization of all the four million and odd trained men[1] in this country into fighting units, of a kind, would be a relatively easy task, for nowadays the power exists (to the hand of the man who knows how to use it) of creating a wave of popular feeling which would sweep all local or individual opposition before it. The essence of the whole matter is that *the man should know his own mind,* and this the average man, whom we may expect to find in

---

1. See the tables in *War and the World's Life* by the author.

authority at any given crisis, never will succeed in doing until he has *steeped himself in the knowledge of what has been done,* and deduced therefrom what can be done again when a great need arises. But this work will be all the easier, the greater the number of the men beneath him trained to view matters from the same standpoint as himself and to realize that after all the Art of War consists, not in striving after unattainable ideals, but in *"making the best practicable use of the means at hand to the attainment of the object in view."*[1]

To return now to the use the Emperor proposed to make of these great masses.

Early in March, he entertained and drafted an outline plan, which though it was never put into execution, deserves notice for the amount of criticism to which it has been subjected, and also because its guiding idea recurs repeatedly at a later stage of this campaign (1813). Leaving a retaining force on the Saale, he proposed to cross the Elbe with his main body, march direct on Berlin and thence relieve the garrisons of the Oder fortresses and Danzig. The chief criticism directed against this has always been, that neither Berlin nor the relief of the fortresses afforded a sufficient objective for a Field Army, which should always aim primarily at the destruction of the Field Army of its adversary, essentially the guiding principle of the whole Napoleonic strategy. Further, it is condemned because it contains no single allusion to the *decisive battle* which all sound strategy should aim at. These criticisms come chiefly from Germany, and I confess that for years they had my full adherence, until I came under the influence of the modern French school, when Napoleon's reasons at once became plain. The chief difficulty of his situation lay in holding, or inducing his enemies to stand, or indeed in controlling their action in any way. The march to Berlin, thence onward, ultimately towards Königsberg, not only meant the ruin of

1. Moltke's definition.

the Prussian Monarchy for a second time, but also threatened the Russian communications with Petersburg. It was, therefore, a reasonable calculation that the threat on Berlin, as once before at Jena, would bring the Allies down in force to oppose it, and marching in his favourite *battalion carrée* it was, as already explained, immaterial to him when, where or how they chose to attack him.

His reason for abandoning the idea has never to my knowledge been made clear. The necessity often alleged for covering the Southern States of Germany to ensure their loyalty has never appealed to me as adequate, because nothing would seem better adapted to secure their wavering attachment than the sight of the beaten Russians and Prussians straggling back upon their frontiers. More probably the scheme was originally based on insufficient information, and was given up when it became clear that the total force the Allies could have concentrated to oppose him was altogether too small to offer them a reasonable prospect of success in the battlefield; therefore they would voluntarily, (abandoning Berlin and East Prussia), fall back into Russia, when he would again find himself face to face with the terrible problem of the previous year, and with far less satisfactory material to enable him to deal with it. At the time of its inception also he had still no adequate idea of the completeness of the disintegration which his old Army had undergone, and he attached far more value to its fragments than they actually deserved. With them the process of «war seasoning» had been overdone, and «war weary» would better describe them. "I have 600 men of the Guard with me here," wrote Rapp from Danzig "but not two hundred will ever be fit for the field again"—and if this was the case with the Guard, the condition of the rest of the Army may be imagined!

Meanwhile, the action of the Allies was forcing Napoleon's hand, and the question of the neutrality of the German Southern States became a matter of time, whilst the attitude of Austria was more than threatening. From Dresden, their advance if continued towards the upper waters of the Saale and Main, covered Bavaria and Saxony, and might even jeopardize the arrival of the IV Corps from Italy via Augsburg. On the other hand, the further they continued in this direction, the more they exposed their own communications to a blow from the north-west, and the chance of catching them in a position in which they would be compelled to fight increased. He, therefore, now busied himself with a plan which was almost the exact inverse of his Jena Campaign, and issued orders to unite his whole force in the angle of the upper Saale and Elbe.

On April 11, the heads of the several Corps had attained their. The Army of the Elbe lay with its Headquarters at Aschersleben—about 30 miles south of Magdeburg. The III Corps along the road from Aschaffenburg to Schweinfurt; VI Corps around Hanau; Guards at Mainz; the IV and XII coming from Italy with their head at Anspach and the rearmost Division ten days' march behind, near Augsburg. The Emperor knew from a certain source that the Russian Guards had only commenced their march from Kalische on April 1, and could not, therefore, reach the troops already in the field before May 1; but it was always possible that the latter might continue their advance without waiting for the Guards, in which case they might reach the Saale by April 20. Therefore, he had to be prepared for this contingency, though it was an improbable one.

Accordingly he prescribed the next stage of his advance in such a manner that his concentration would be assured whatever case arose. To this end the Army of the Elbe was directed to advance to the line of the Wipper—a small affluent of the Saale, with its left resting on the latter river and its right on the slopes of the Harz Mountains, thus threatening the enemy's right if they should attempt to march upon Erfurt. The VI Corps and Guards were to move along the great road from Mainz through Fulda, Gotha, to Erfurt, the III Corps from Schweinfurt to Meiningen, and the IV and XII Corps by Bamberg, Coburg, and Grafenthal.

The Emperor had caused most careful reconnaissances to be made of all the roads through the Thuringian forest—a mountainous densely wooded district with ridges rising some 3,000 feet above the plain. He knew that from Meiningen and Coburg alternative roads existed which would enable him either to direct the further movement of these Corps on Erfurt or on the Saale, as the case might require. If now the Allies determined to march either direct upon Erfurt or against the Army of the Elbe, in either case the latter could hold them till the centre and right swung in—or if by the time they reached the above-mentioned places it was clear that the enemy was moving southward against the right column, or waiting for the Russian Guards to arrive—the whole of his forces could combine their forward movement, and complete their concentration in the neighbourhood of Leipzig; and this was what actually happened.

On April 24 it was clear that no further interference with the French concentration about Leipzig was to be anticipated. The Army of the Elbe still lay on the Wipper, the III Corps at Weimar, followed by the Guards, which had passed the VI Corps at Erfurt, and the VI strung out along the road from Gotha to Vacha for some 30 miles. The IV and XII Corps lay with their advance guard at Grafenthal, their main body extending from Coburg to Anspach. The Bavarians were on the extreme right at Bayreuth, the total front being about 140 miles, depth 60 miles. But the Emperor himself had delayed too long at Mainz, trusting to his Generals on the spot, and as usual they had fallen far short of his reasonable expectations. Ney, having reached Meiningen, and not having appreciated Napoleon's reason for ordering him to make a temporary halt at that place, had concluded, that as the road from Meiningen to Weimar across the hills was rather an indifferent one, he would take the easy one down the valley to Eisenach, and cut in on the main road through Erfurt to that place. He thus fouled the line of march of the Guards and VI Corps, blocking them back all along the road.

At the same time the Cavalry of the Allies made a succession of brilliant attacks in the district between the Wipper and Unstrutt with the result that a series of regrettable incidents, from the French point of view, took place. On April 12, Major Blücher (son of the Field-Marshal) at the head of some 200 Prussian Hussars appeared before Weimar, with this result, that the Saxon Battalion on duty immediately laid down its arms. On the 17th, Major Helwig with a Squadron of 150 men fell suddenly upon the rearguard of the Bavarian Division (Rechberg) near Langen-Salza, capturing some hundred men and a couple of guns. On the 18th the same party dispersed a Westphalian Cavalry regiment, near Wanried on the road to Cassel, thus creating wild alarm in King Jerome's mind. Finally, reports of all these events reaching Ney at Erfurt on the 19th, caused him serious apprehension of more to follow. The result was a series of orders and counter-orders which narrowly escaped throwing the whole command into disorder. As Marshal Bessières wrote to Berthier:

> I must tell you frankly that if the enemy had been advancing on Naumburg and Jena as the Prince de la Moskova wrote to me that night, we should have been in no position to meet them, or the Prince either.

Meanwhile the Emperor's orders were already on their way for the whole Army to concentrate on the Saale on April 25.

> The Army of the Main marches on Jena and Naumburg; the Army of the Elbe will move up the Saale and occupy Halle and Merseburg. The Corps from Italy, if circumstances permit, will march by Saalfeld on Jena, by the left bank of the Saale.

In elucidation of this the Major General (Berthier), wrote to Prince Eugène from Mainz (April 22):

> The Emperor is to-day still in Mainz. As the Corps of the Prince de la Moskova cannot be completely closed up until the 24th, it is necessary for you to occupy Querfurt so as to maintain direct communication with the Prince, who is going to occupy the heights above Naumburg. Destroy the bridge which the enemy has over the Saale near Wettin. Occupy Halle and Merseburg as bridge heads, and place these towns in a condition of defence against Cossacks by palisading the gates. Occupy Halle first, Merseburg afterwards. *The Emperor's intention is to guard the whole of the Saale, so that the enemy cannot penetrate to the left bank at any spot.* You must be on the alert to march at once against the enemy should he advance from Jena or Naumburg.

Following closely upon these orders, the Emperor himself reached Erfurt on the morning of the 25th April, and the first duty to claim his attention was the arrangements of the Supply Service. The Corps had taken the field with from 12 to 14 days' bread, biscuit or meal—four days' rations carried by the men, the remainder in carts, and they had lived as far as possible on the country they had traversed. But now they were too concentrated to do this, and were to be fed from the magazines Napoleon had ordered to be prepared in Erfurt. Evidently this service had been neglected, for on the evening of the 25th we find a letter to Marshal Duroc.

> Collect tonight the Intendant and two or three of the principal members of the administration of the country, as well as the Commissary of War, and settle what steps are to be taken to collect supplies at Erfurt. We must have in four days 200,000 rations of bread to issue at the rate of 50,000 a day. They must also procure as soon as

possible, two million rations of flour—as much beef on the hoof and brandy; also two million rations of oats. To get these quicker you are to pay cash.

The main line of communication for the Main Army was to be by Mainz, Fulda, Gotha, while the IV and XII Corps after passing Saalfeld were to give up completely their previous line, *viz.*, Coburg and Nuremburg; and any communications necessary with Augsburg were to go by Fulda-Wurzburg, an indication of the growing insecurity of the country. A comparison of the halting places actually attained with the orders issued, shows that in the Army of the Main all the prescribed marches were duly and punctually performed, but the Army of the Elbe was 24 hours late in starting and then only averaged seven miles a day. No explanation of this extraordinary slowness is forthcoming, but it is worth while to note in passing that, with Napoleon in person on the spot, twenty-five, even thirty miles a day was by no means an unusual effort for bodies of such strength to accomplish. Singularly, also, there is no trace of any reprimand being administered to Eugene for this dilatoriness.

On the 30th, the several Corps attained the under-mentioned positions.

Army of the Main

Headquarters of the Emperor		Weissenfels
The Imperial Guard		Weissenfels
III Corps	Headquarters and four Divisions	East of Weissenfels
	Marchand's Division	Stossen
VI Corps	Headquarters and two Divisions	Naumburg
	Friedrich's Division	Kösen
IV Corps		Along the Saale from Dornburg to Jena and Rudolstadt

XII Corps	Still in rear, between Saalfeld and Coburg

The Army of the Elbe

Headquarters and Division Roguet (Guards)	Merseburg
1st Cavalry Corps and XI Corps	Three miles east of Merseburg
V Corps	Three Divisions west of Merseburg; a detachment of four Battalions at Halle
32nd Division	at Schafstedt
4th Division (Victor):	Bernburg

The ten Battalions of this Division formed a cordon all along the Saale, which river was henceforth so closely watched that none of the enemy's Cavalry succeeded in crossing it. *This cordon defence of a river line was Napoleon's expedient to compensate for his deficiency in Cavalry, for it gave him "security" and ensured secrecy of his own movements,* but of course it could not help him to ascertain what his enemy was about. For this, however, he cared little; he had now 145,000 men in hand ready to fight in any direction at a moment's notice, and it mattered nothing to him when or where he met his opponents, if only they would fight to a finish when they did encounter him. Secrecy and promptitude were, however, the essential factors of the situation, for if once the Allies realized the overwhelming numbers against them, they would certainly concentrate to the rear, as for the moment they had no interest in the actual occupation of the ground on which they stood. Experience had shown them the efficacy of a rapid retreat as a means of evading Napoleon's sledge hammer blows.

Napoleon's His orders, therefore, for May 1, ran as follows:

The Army of the Elbe is to advance in front of Merseburg to Schladebach—placing Merseburg in a condition of defence.

The III Corps with the Cavalry of the Guard from Weissenfels towards Lützen.

The VI Corps to support the III with two Divisions, the third remaining at Naumburg. The Imperial Guard (two Division) to Weissenfels.

The IV and XII to continue towards Naumburg as rapidly as possible.

As this movement took the Army out into open country very favourable for the enemy's Cavalry, to avoid any possibility of surprise, the troops now marched in masses straight across country.

The formation of the III Corps may be taken as the type generally followed. Behind an Advance Guard consisting of all the Corps Cavalry (a Brigade of 10 Squadrons), two Battalions and a half Battery of Light Artillery, the Main Body followed at a distance of about 3,000 yards in as many lines as it contained Brigades. Each Brigade was in line of columns of Regiments (four Battalions) with double company front at half distance, so as to be able to form regimental squares rapidly. The Artillery of each Division between the leading Brigades.

As Napoleon had expected, the Cavalry of the Allies attempted several charges during the day, but were easily repulsed with a trifling loss. There was no longer a Seydlitz to lead them, nor were they trained to that great Leader's standard of perfection; and the day would have ended most satisfactorily but for the unfortunate death of Marshal Bessières, killed dead by a cannon shot at the passage of the Rippach. The bearing of the young soldiers had won the approval even of Ney, who with many others seems at first to have had serious doubts as to their steadiness. At the close of the day the Emperor was at Lützen.

Army of the Elbe

XI Corps		from Quentz to Markranstädt
V Corps		in rear of Gunthendorf
1st Cavalry Corps		between Schladebach and Oetzach
	32nd Division	at Merseburg

Army of the Main

Cavalry of the Guard		at Lützen
Imperial Guard		(two Divisions) Weissenfels
III Corps	Headquarters	Kaja
	Souham's Division	Kaja, Rahna, Klein and Grosz Gorschen
	Girard's Division	Starsiedel
	Brennier's Division	near Lützen
	Ricard's Division	near Lützen
	Marchand's Division	near Lützen
VI Corps	Headquarters	near Rippach
	Bouet's Division	near Rippach
	Compans Division	near Lösau, west of Rippach
	Freidrichs' Division	at Naumburg
IV Corps	Headquarters	Stössen
	Morand's Division	Stössen; Advance Guard: Pretzsch
	Peyri's Division	Grosz-Gestewitz
	Wurtemberg Division	Jena
XII Corps		Head of Column at Kahla, rear near Saalfeld

On the left the flank being protected by the Elbe and Elster, needs no particular precaution, so the whole left and centre are closed up to form the "mass of manœuvre"—the right flank being covered by the III Corps and Guards, from Weissenfels to Lützen, whilst the IV Corps from Stössen to Jena is in a position to outflank any attack upon the III coming from the southward.

From the reports of the enemy's movements received, it appeared that the latter was concentrating about Zwenkau, whilst a portion of his troops still held Leipzig. Judging from his knowledge of Wittgenstein's character, the Emperor considered an attack on his right flank during the next day as highly probable. But this threat did not deter him an instant in his determination to gain ground to the front and appear in mass in the plains to the east of the Elster on May 3.

As a measure of precaution, however, the III Corps around Lützen was ordered to stand fast till noon, whilst the Army of the Elbe advanced on Leipzig, and all other elements of the Army closed in on the III Corps.

In case of an attack from Zwenkau the III Corps is thus facing in the required direction to act as Advance Guard— to fix the enemy and allow the remainder of the Army to manœuvre against him.

Kaja is about 13 miles from Leipzig, 16 miles from Markranstädt, 5 from Rippach, 10 from Weissenfels, and 14 from Stössen. The III Corps 45,000 strong, is therefore amply sufficient to hold its ground until reinforcements arrive, and in six hours at latest the whole Army, 145,000 men—less the Division ordered to Leipzig, will be actually deployed in line of battle.

In their execution of these orders the troops had reached position, when about 11 a.m. a tremendous cannonade burst out in the direction of Kaja, and Napoleon leaving the Army of the Elbe to continue its movement, galloped across country to see what had happened.

Reaching the brow of a low undulation which hid the field of action from his sight, he suddenly discovered Souham's Division (part of it already in serious disorder), beset by overwhelming forces of the enemy. Souham's troops had allowed themselves to be surprised in broad daylight by almost the whole of their adversary's Army.

The Emperor was not disconcerted even for a moment. Taking the whole situation in at a glance, he issued the following terse and fitting orders.

The III Corps will hold its position *at any cost. Its business is to fix the enemy, and thus form a pivot on which the rest of the Army can manoeuvre.*

The VI Corps prolongs the right of the III Corps.

The IV Corps moves against the enemy's left.

The XI and 1st Cavalry Corps against his right.

The V Corps occupies Leipzig with one of its Divisions, the others to be echeloned near Markranstädt ready to move on Kaja.

The Guard marches to the sound of the guns.

Here we will leave him and return to the doings of the Allies which had led to this surprise.

We saw them last on April 19, just at the of the moment when a premature rumour of the arrival of the Emperor at the front compelled them to decide on a course of action.

At this date the Corps of Miloradowitch was moving from Dresden to join Blücher at Altenburg, where he had been since the 14th of the month, and the Russian Guards were still five marches to the west of Dresden. The news of the death of Kutusow had just been received, and Wittgenstein appointed to the Command-in-chief of the whole Army. At this date, inclusive of the troops already on the Saale, it consisted of 65,000 Infantry, 22,000 Cavalry, 8,000 Artillery with 450 guns.

A rearward movement of concentration would undoubtedly have been the best plan to adopt from a strictly military point of view, but to withdraw without even the show of a fight would have been politically disastrous, in view of the attitude of Austria and the state of public feeling all over Germany. Moreover, the Prussian troops were still too raw to stand the strain of a prolonged retreat. A defeat in battle even if accompanied by heavy losses, might, in the exalted condition of patriotism in which they found themselves, be far better for their subsequent cohesion than the depressing influences of a continuous withdrawal. Finally, in view of the reports that had reached them, as to the poor condition of the French Cavalry and conscripts, both Blücher, Yorck and Wittgenstein felt that with 22,000 horsemen behind them, in a theatre of rolling plains especially favourable to their action, the chances in favour of a victory were good enough to justify the risk. The only point unsettled was the best point of concentration to select. Wittgenstein had rightly gauged the intention of Napoleon to advance through Leipzig, and had called up Blücher from the south to Borna, whilst he himself had determined to concentrate between Leipzig and Würzen. But the Emperor Alexander, who arrived at this moment, considered that this disposition rendered it probable that, in case of disaster, the whole Army would be thrown back on the Elbe about Torgau —and he decided on a more southerly position between Leipzig and Borna.

They were in this position when, in the course of May 1, the reports of Cavalry—most accurate as to what could actually be seen—led them to conclude that the whole French Army was moving in one long column on Leipzig, hardly guarding their right flank at all. And the opportunity to take advantage of this negligence was too tempting to be allowed to escape them. This conclusion, though in fact erroneous, was an almost inevitable consequence of the failure of the Allied Generals to penetrate the real secret of the Napoleonic methods.

Accordingly, leaving Kleist in Leipzig to hold the town (a semi-mediaeval fortress) to the last, orders were issued at 11.30 p.m. on May 1, to the following effect:

The Corps of Miloradowitch (12,000 men) on Zeitz to watch in the direction of Naumburg and Jena.

The Corps Winzingerode (12,000men), to Werben, to cover the passage of the main Army over the Elster and Flossgraben.

The Corps of Blücher (27,000 men) in two columns to cross the Elster at Storkwitz and Pegau.

The Corps of Yorck (7,500 men) passes the Elster at Pegau, after Blücher's left column., the troops of Berg at Storkwitz behind the right.

The Guards(18,500 men) follows the troops of Yorck and Berg.

The Army will form up beyond the Flossgraben, the right on the canal near Werben, and the left at Grünabach near Sohesten, the movement to be completed by 7 a.m.

The troops were on the march between 1 and 2 a.m. (they were, therefore, probably awaiting the arrival of the above orders), but from want of clearness in their instructions, the columns crossed one another, and the resulting delays postponed the final deployment till 11 a.m. The Army then stood in three lines, hidden by a roll of the ground, some 2,000 yards south of Gross Gorschen. Owing to the long night march, the men were much exhausted, and it was decided to allow them another hour's rest. Meanwhile Wittgenstein, with the Headquarters Staff, rode forward to a mound about 1,200 yards south of Gross Gorschen, whence they saw great clouds of dust hanging heavily over the main road to Leipzig, and in the immediate foreground were a large mass of French troops cooking their dinners and completely off their guard.

This was Souham's Division of Ney's Corps waiting for further orders, and what followed was an exact anticipation of the opening of so many actions in the 1870 campaign—notably that of Vionville, both sides making the same mistakes.

The whole Army of the Allies being already deployed, it would have sufficed to launch a Cavalry Division on Souham to overwhelm all opposition, and then to advance over the wreck of the French Advance Guard with the whole of the Artillery and Infantry on a broad front, crushing each fresh echelon of the enemy as it came on the ground. Instead of this, the Allies grew circumspect, and advancing some 36 guns, opened the attack with a single Brigade, and the first shots fired gave the alarm to the whole of the French Army.

The first rush of the Prussians easily carried Gross Gorschen, but when they endeavoured to throw a mass of 23 Squadrons on the retreating French—a line of Batteries came rapidly into action between Rahna and Klein Gorschen, and brought the former to a stop with case shot. Then Girard's Division arrived on the spot, and immediately afterwards the whole of the VI Corps (Marmont) came up on his right about Starsiedel, so that by 10 p.m. about 40,000 French were in action against some 65,000 of the Allies. Then followed a series of disconnected and successive attacks by Brigades, where whole Army Corps would have been more to the purpose, and after desperate fighting the villages of Rahna and Klein Gorschen also fell into the hands of the Allies, who then prepared to push forward on Kaja, where Ney in person had in the meantime arrived. Placing himself at the head of Brenier's Division, on whom the remains of Girard's and Souham's commands at once rallied, Ney led them forward, and with the bayonet drove the Allies back to Rahna and Klein Gorschen. Again the Prussians threw in another Brigade, and in turn the French gave way.

At 2.30 Napoleon rode up to Kaja with the Guards. His arrival produced an extraordinary effect on his troops, who saluted him "with cries of *'Vive l'Empereur,'* in which even the wounded and dying joined" *(vide* testimony of von Odeleben, a Saxon officer on Napoleon's staff). Instantly taking in the situation, he sent his A.D.C., General Mouton, to Ricard's

Division (the last closed reserve of the III Corps), with orders to execute a counter attack, and again bearing down all opposition, the French became masters of the two villages.

Meanwhile, the Cavalry and Cossacks of the Allies had been thundering down in a succession of disunited charges on Marmont's Infantry, and the Marshal, impressed by the visible masses of the enemy in front of him, sent to Napoleon for reinforcements.

The reply he received was characteristic:"Tell your Marshal he is mistaken, the decision lies at Kaja, not at Starsiedel."

A lull in the battle now set in, only the Artillery on both sides continued their fire, and meanwhile Wittgenstein, learning of the approach of the IV and XI Corps, prepared for a final effort. The moment was critical for Napoleon—it was about 4.30 p.m.—the III Corps was practically burnt out and useless, the VI could not be moved, as its presence at Starsiedel was imperative to protect the flank of the III Corps, and only the Guards were available on the spot. But he hesitated to engage them, because he saw that *the battle was not yet ripe*, i.e. that the enemy had not yet expended all his reserves and reached that crisis of nervous exhaustion on which the success of the aggressor's final blow depends.

At this moment, about 4.30, some Battalions of the III Corps broke. The Emperor galloped into the middle of them, rallied them by the sheer magnetic power of his personality (none who lived through this moment could ever forget it), and sending in a Brigade of the Young Guard to give them a lead, led back the whole III Corps into the fight. On no occasion in his whole career did Napoleon expose himself more recklessly, and never had his extraordinary power of command asserted itself to a greater extent. It was not, and could not be the mere example of personal courage. In an Army numbering such men as Ney, Mouton, and Rapp in its ranks, personal courage in itself would hardly have attracted unusual attention. It was the indefinable something in the man himself that reawakened the confidence and enthusiasm of all ranks, which, to put it gently, had slumbered somewhat during the months succeeding his hurried departure from Smorgoni on December 14, 1812.

This must be borne in mind throughout the whole of this campaign, if the extraordinary heroism of the French troops immediately under his eyes is to be understood and explained.

At last towards 5 p.m. the XI Corps preceded by all its Artillery (60 guns), began to arrive from the direction of Eisdorf and Kitzen, reaching well round the enemy's right wing, and at the same time Morand's Division of the IV Corps appeared upon their left.

The time had now come for the final "knock out" blow, and Drouot with sixty guns of the Guard Artillery galloped out to the front, and unlimbering at case shot range, began to tear the very heart out of the Allied Army, whilst the whole Infantry of the Guard followed in rear, sweeping along with it all that still had life in the sorely shattered III Corps. The Allies gave way at all points, but the blow had been timed a little too late, and in the absence of an efficient Cavalry, darkness intervened to prevent the victorious Infantry reaping their full reward.

To cover their retreat, the Cavalry of the Allies made several gallant charges, and finally just before midnight, a party of eleven squadrons, under a Colonel Dolfs, in the midst of complete darkness, over difficult ground, and guided only by the bivouac fires, threw themselves into the very heart of the French lines. What followed has never been quite clearly established. The French deny all panics, the Prussians affirm them; all that is certain is that the French were kept under arms all night, and morning found them too completely worn out to pursue.

No more striking contrast, illustrating the difference of the fighting value between troops raised under the old long service conditions, fighting for "the honour of their arms" and those raised under the new, inspired primarily by a feeling of nationality, can well be desired than is presented by the different conduct of the Prussians on this occasion and at Jena. The Army of Jena, with a Man at the head of it, would probably have overwhelmed the III and VI Corps in an hour (as Frederick the Great had overwhelmed Soubise barely sixty years before within twenty miles of the same spot), then with the impetus of success on its side it would have swept the remainder before it. It would certainly have stood up to far heavier punishment on the field, for compared with Torgau, Zorndorf, and Kunersdorf,[1] the losses at Gross Gorschen (or Lützen as the French call it) were not severe; but once beaten, they would have dissolved, precisely as they had done at Jena and Auerstädt. The new Prussian Army, though badly beaten, *refused* to dissolve. Every man wanted to get back to his own Battalion; and not having lost all sense of locality by many years' confinement to the barrack yard and one mile beyond it, even a dark night proved but little obstacle to their doing so. In a surprisingly short time the stragglers had sorted themselves out, and were well on their way from the field, and when next morning dawned not a single gun or trophy of any kind remained as prizes for the victorious French.

This was a most fatal blow to the Imperial prestige, for it entirely obscured the remarkable strategy that had united about 140,000 men on the battlefield, but called attention to the fact that these 140,000 odd had not achieved sufficient success against the 75,000 of the allies to bring in a single gun or other trophy. All other conditions which might be brought forward to palliate this want of success, *i.e.* want of Cavalry, the darkness of the night, etc., were overlooked in the general rejoicing in every Foreign Ministry in Europe over this striking contrast between Napoleon's previous victories and that of Lützen.

---

1. Prussian losses at Torgau 29·8 percent., Zorndorf 37·5 percent., Kunersdorf 48·2 per cent.

Nor had the Emperor better reason to be pleased with the fighting quality which his men had shown. He had actually engaged three Corps, about 60,000 men, had expended one completely, and but for his arrival in person on the scene with the Guard, there could be no doubt that both the VI and III Corps, together with any other Corps in the Army except the Guard, would have been completely defeated under any of his Marshals. Yet the Allies had not engaged the whole of their forces, for (apart from Bülow, who away to the north near Halle had been left out of the combination entirely) Miloradowitch, delayed on the march by causes no longer possible of elucidation, had failed to reach the battlefield before the resolution to retreat had been taken.

It will be noticed also that throughout the day the Allies were on interior lines relatively to the French, yet even with the additional advantage of surprise on their side, this could not save them. Had Wittgenstein's original proposal to concentrate about Würzen been adhered to, they would then have been outside the horns of the attack, with the whole Corps of Bülow, (inclusive of Kleist) available, and might then have entertained the reasonable expectation of crushing the heads of the French columns as they defiled across extemporized crossings over the Elster, and out of the narrow gates of Leipzig. This is assuming that Kleist had abandoned that place of his own free will, without any adequate garrison, a course he had no reason to adopt, since poor though its fortifications undoubtedly were, 5,000 men could have held it for days against an Army unprovided with a siege train.

It has been pointed out above that the old Prussian Army would have attacked *en masse* and overwhelmed the III Corps in its first rush. This marks a very important difference between the guiding ideas of the post-Revolutionary tactics and those of the Frederickian era, and deserves more attention than it has yet received, since it involves the whole theory of the use of reserves in battle.

The fundamental conception underlying the old Line tactics lay in the idea of *overwhelming the enemy by a single crushing blow,* in contradistinction to the plan of *wearing him down by attrition.* The same idea still underlies the employment of Cavalry in action, and may be justified by the following reasoning. If we imagine the "Line," whether of Foot or Horse, to move forward as an irresistible scythe of death, exterminating every living thing lying within its swathe, it is quite clear that Reserves following behind it would be useless, except perhaps to collect and bury the dead.[1]

No "Line" has ever quite attained this utmost expression of destructive power—but the old "Line" of Frederick the Great's Infantry, giving its four regular volleys a minute, or Seydlitz's Squadrons sweeping down "knee behind knee" not merely "boot to boot" *(see* von der Marwitz) made a very close approximation to this ideal, and the nearer it was approached the fewer the Reserves that either required. But for the attainment of this ideal, the highest possible skill was needed in every individual concerned, from the Divisional General down to the private, and this skill the short training which was available under the new conditions imported by the Revolution could not supply.

Hence the necessity for heavy reserves became apparent, and in time this provision of reserves came to be regarded as the essential point, and *not the provision of an all-destroying "Line."* But prevision to meet its inevitable shortcomings was also most necessary.

For nearly twenty years the French had been almost uniformly successful when fighting in this form, *i.e.* skirmishers and heavy reserves, hence the conclusion seemed obvious that in the form itself lay the secret of their victories, and

---

1. *See* note at end of chapter.

not in the causes which led to the evolution of the form. Hence all Europe, except Great Britain, had copied it, and when the opportunity arose to employ the old form, viz. the Frederickian "Line," to its utmost advantage, the spirit of the latter had been lost, and only the letter of the new regulation remained.

Even now, nearly a century afterwards, the letter of the "Reserves" form still rules, and there is not in Europe an Army trained to seize such an opportunity should it again be offered. But human nature remains human nature no matter how much weapons may change, and this being the case such opportunities will again arise, and a wise preparation for War would see to it that the troops taking part in it could be employed to the best advantage.

The essence of the whole matter may be summed up in this. If a General is to control the situation, no matter how or when it arises, then his soldiers must be trained to execute his wishes; in other words, they must be sufficiently "drilled," even in whole Army Corps if necessary. If the troops are only "trained" in accordance with the current conception of what a battle should be, then when an emergency comes the Army controls the General, which is putting the cart before the horse. This was the spirit of the old Peninsular Army, and this it was that Wellington meant when he said that with it he "was prepared to go anywhere and do anything."

The losses of the day, though, as above mentioned, relatively small compared with those of the Seven Years' War, were nevertheless quite sensible. While the Allies owned to 10,000 the French had to admit 18,000 killed, wounded, or prisoners, 12,000 of which were in the III Corps alone, and it thus lost 25 per cent, of its Infantry. But whereas the young French conscripts, fighting without a cause which appealed to them, reported themselves as sick or wounded on the smallest excuse, the young Prussians, fully saturated with the importance of the stakes for which they fought, stuck to the ranks as long as their legs could carry them. The Russians also have never been good malingerers, their Company was and is their home, and their ambulances held no attraction for them.

Note.—Compare Lord Lake's tactics at the battle on the Hindun near Delhi, September 11, 1803. The Mahrattas hold a very strong position, numerous batteries sweeping the ground with their fire up to extreme range. Lake's Infantry attacked in a single deployed line—his Cavalry alone available as a Reserve—and checking only to fire a single volley, carried the position with the bayonet.— See Pearse's *Life and Military Services of Viscount Lake.*

CHAPTER 5

From Lützen to the Armistice

Under cover of Miloradowitch's intact command (12,000 men) and the Cavalry, the Allies rallied their troops which had been engaged, on Frohburg and Borna, and then decided to continue their retreat, the Prussians by Colditz and Meissen, the Russians by Rochlitz, on Dresden. Parks and convoys by Freiburg and Chemnitz ultimately on Dresden also. Büllow, near Halle, charged with the special mission of covering Berlin, was informed of their intentions and invited to withdraw behind the Elbe at Rosslau.

As soon as order could be restored in the French ranks the Emperor pressed on in pursuit, but here his want of Cavalry told severely, and, over and above his deficiency in this respect, lay the hopeless corruption and inefficiency of his Supply Department. Since the men could draw no rations, they broke up to forage for themselves, and presently this evil attained the most serious dimensions. Thus in a report of the Provost Marshal dated May 15, 1813, quoted by Col. Lanrezac (p. 170) we find that flying columns sent in to collect stragglers had found no less than 5,200 between the Elsters and the Elbe, three-quarters of which, it is only fair to the French to record, were Italians of the IV and XII Corps, neither of which had been actually under fire. The following order speaks for itself:

Ordre du Jour
May 6, 1813

Many soldiers have wandered into the country to right and left of the road, others follow the columns as stragglers. It is the fault of the officers who allow the men to leave the ranks. It is the fault of the Generals who march without rear guards to pick up the stragglers. The soldiers unload their arms by firing them off, instead of using the cleaning stick to draw the charge. Others roam about the fields firing at the cattle. This is a crime; because in War a gun shot is frequently the signal of alarm. It is also a crime, because the bullet might kill or wound persons by accident; finally it is a crime because it is an act of maraud. His Majesty orders that any soldier who fires off his musket either as a marauder or to save himself the trouble of unloading properly, shall be punished by imprisonment and degradation. If the shot wounds or kills any one, he shall be punished by death.

Alexandre
Prince de Neuchatel
Major-General

The Army of the Elbe not having been engaged in the battle, and being also nearest to Dresden and the Elbe, was sent on in pursuit of the enemy, but again the Viceroy's incurable slowness called down upon him the Emperor's reprimands. It seems that the custom had crept in of allowing an indefinite number of private wagons and carriages to accompany the troops, and for second line transport to be inserted in the columns between the combatant Divisions. To put a stop to this abuse, orders were issued that any private vehicles found in the columns would be burnt, and their horses handed over to the Artillery. Only the Artillery wagons were to march with their Divisions, and the rest of the baggage was relegated to the tail of the columns. Fortunately for the French, the Allies were in no hurry to evacuate the ground they held, and soon the pursuers were in touch with rear guards of all arms on the roads towards Dresden and the Elbe, but it was not at first clear by which road the bulk of their forces had moved. Napoleon, therefore, pressed for prisoners, but the admirable order in which the retreat was conducted made it difficult for his subordinates to comply with the demand. At Colditz, on May 4, the XI Corps came upon a Prussian rear guard, and after a sharp tussle, the latter retired, leaving only some twenty or thirty prisoners behind it. The Emperor's reply to the Viceroy's report of this action is characteristic:

> My Son,
> Yesterday's would have been a very pretty affair had you sent me 3,000 prisoners. How is it that in a hilly and wooded country where the enemy's Cavalry are useless, you cannot catch any for me? The Duke of Ragusa marches for Waldheim at 4 a.m. tomorrow. Take good care to move off not later than 5 a.m., and close up your columns so as not to occupy more than three leagues (nine miles) of road. Place all your baggage at the end of your 3rd Division, so as to march in a soldier-like manner, and be able to bring the whole of your three Divisions into action simultaneously. Put a little order into your Corps; it wants it badly. The Italians in particular commit atrocities, robbing and pillaging wherever they go. Shoot a few of them.
> *Your affectionate father*

The reports received on the night of May 4 made it clear that the Russians and Prussians were retreating on Dresden and Meissen, but the strength and whereabouts of Bülow's troops to the northward were still in doubt. In any case it was not and could not be clear whether the Allies would endeavour to hold the Une of the Elbe, whether they would cross the Elbe, then separate, the Prussians retiring on Berlin, the Russians to Silesia, or whether the two combined would continue their retreat in the latter direction. Moreover, Napoleon appears to have been obsessed with the idea that the King of Prussia attached particular importance to the possession of Berlin, and he also seems to have been unable to rid his mind of the thought of relieving the Oder fortresses; a proceeding which would only have set free the investing forces by which their garrisons were held in check. According to rule these could not well be less than three times the strength of the troops they neutralized.

With a double object before him, he therefore decided to form a new Army, under Marshal Ney, out of Ney's own Corps the III, the II provisional Corps under Victor, the VII under Reynier, and another provisional command under Sebastiani which consisted of Puthod's Division of the V Corps, and the 2nd Cavalry Corps, both of which were still on the Lower Elbe. With this command Ney was to cross the Elbe at Torgau, and hold himself ready to move either up the right bank of the Elbe to Dresden or direct on Berlin as circumstances might dictate.

The Emperor seems to have counted on Saxon cooperation from the first, for Reynier's Corps on paper comprised the two Saxon Divisions, at that time forming under General Thielman the garrison of Torgau, and he was disagreeably surprised when on May 7 news reached him that Torgau refused to open its gates, alleging specific orders from the King of Saxony, and simultaneously that the King himself had abandoned Dresden and withdrawn to Prague, taking with him all his heavy bodyguard Cavalry. Prague being in Austrian territory made the matter doubly awkward.

A messenger of the Diplomatic Staff was at once sent post haste after the fugitive, with an ultimatum giving the King six hours to decide whether he would adhere to the affiance still existing between himself and the Emperor, order Torgau to surrender, at once and return to his capital, or see Dresden and his country treated as conquered territory forthwith.

Meanwhile the Allies were resolutely contesting every mile of the French advance, and the operations of Miloradowitch's column are a model for rear guard Commanders to study. Only a resolute push from the southward by the IV Corps could have hastened matters, but this was one of the Italian Corps, and its men were poor marchers, from want of sufficient discipline. On August 8 the advance guard of the French Army with the Emperor's Headquarters entered Dresden; only to see the last of the Russian troops filing over the bridge to the Neustadt, the suburb on the right bank of the Elbe, and immediately afterwards two spans of the bridge were blown into the air, leaving gaps of 140 feet to repair. Unfortunately for the Allies, the demolition charges were put in too high up, thus the lower tiers of the bridge piles were left untouched, and the work of reconstruction was markedly facilitated.

The French had taken six days to cover 80 miles, an average which fell far short of Napoleon's usual idea of a day's march in pursuit, *viz.* seven to eight leagues, *i.e.* 21 to 24 miles.

All the boats on the river had been systematically destroyed or removed, and though the *pontonniers* were at hand, the pontoons were still fifteen marches in the rear. Hence recourse had to be taken to rafts of timber and other improvised material, which led to many delays. Even anchors had to be improvised out of rough timber cases filled with stones. The Emperor, finding it impossible to reconstruct the main bridge in face of the Russian guns and musketry from the Neustadt, decided to force a passage lower down the river at a convenient re-entering bend near Briesnitz; and this gave rise to one of the classic examples of the passage of a river under fire. The Russians held the opposite bank with Infantry and some sixty guns, but the French brought up eighty, and taking the whole salient bend of the stream, and the plain beyond it, under a convergent fire, soon obtained a fire superiority, under cover of which a few parties of Infantry were first put across. Then the *pontonniers*, sheltered by the actual bank of the river from direct vision, managed to float their rafts into position and complete the roadway. *(See* Sir Howard Douglas' *Military Bridges,* for details.)

At the same time another attempt to secure a footing on

the right bank at Neustadt was made. Twenty guns unlimbered on the well-known terrace of Brühl, and protected by their fire, 300 Voltigeurs of the Guard managed to cross on the few boats which had escaped the general destruction, and seized a strongly built stone building covering the exit from the permanent bridge. Upon this the Russians began to evacuate the suburb, seemingly without sufficient justification. The repair of the bridge was at once put in hand, and on the afternoon of the 10th, a few men of Charpentier's Division passed the principal breach in the bridge by means of long fire-escape ladders.

As soon as it became clear that the passage at Briesnitz had been won, orders were issued to the XI, IV and VI Corps to prepare to cross on the morrow (May 10). But in the night a flood came down the river, carrying with it great quantities of drift wood, the bridge was swept away, and a further delay of some thirty-six hours was thus occasioned.

For the moment, therefore, the outlook for the French was gloomy, for not a single standing bridge over the river was in their hands. Besides which the same flood that had swept away the bridge at Briesnitz had increased their difficulties everywhere else. Fortunately, the messenger despatched to the King of Saxony at Prague returned very opportunely with orders to Thielman to hand over the fortress of Torgau.

Accordingly, during the course of May 11, troops entered the town and Reynier was at last in a position to take over his two Saxon Divisions.

This move, however, did not pass off without friction. Thielman, who was most bitterly opposed to the French had left for Dresden before they arrived, and throughout the period of his command he had done his best to promote a German spirit amongst his men and officers, therefore a good deal of re-organization was necessary before the Saxons could be induced to march under their new masters. Reynier's report to Ney (given in *Foucart,* p. 137) is amusing in its querulousness, and his troubles did not end there, because an epidemic, "nervous fever" (probably influenza) had broken out, so that it was inadvisable to quarter troops in the town. Neither Victor's nor Sebastiani's Corps had arrived, they were indeed still some seven days' march away, their advance being constantly harassed by partisan raids based on Büllow's Corps, and it was fortunate that the Allies had already set out on their further retreat, as Ney had only Durutte's Division of the VII Corps and his own III Corps, of reliable troops, at his disposal.

Much ill feeling had developed between the Prussians and Russians during the retreat to Dresden, of which Napoleon was kept duly informed by rumours collected by his advance patrols. It seems that this ill feeling had penetrated even to the Supreme Command, for the Prussians actually began their march on May 9, from Meissen on Groszenhayn, *i.e.* towards Berlin, whilst the Russians from Neustadt took the road to Radeberg and Breslau. But on the 10th wiser counsels prevailed, and leaving the protection of Berlin to Bülow and his partisans, King Frederick William directed his troops, by the road through Kamenz towards Bautzen, where the Russians had preceded him. Here the two Sovereigns decided to make a further stand, and proceeded to fortify their position.

Napoleon's Headquarters remained in Dresden from May 8-17, the time being utilized to re-organize his troops and incorporate into the several Corps the reinforcements completed since the opening of hostilities, and now on their way to join him.

On May 12, Prince Eugene received the following order, which those who have followed his progress so far must admit to have been fully deserved:

My Son
Start tonight for Munich, and from thence proceed to Italy, where you will take over the command of all my troops in that country, and the Illyrian Provinces. It is my intention to form an Army of observation of between eighty and ninety Battalions, half French, half Italian.

The Army of the Elbe was now broken up, its Corps being absorbed by the Grand Army under the personal command of the Emperor. The following table gives its composition on May 15.

	Divisions.	Batts.	Squdrns.	Batteries.	Men.
IV Corps Bertrand	Morand (French) . . . / Peyri (Italian) . . . / Franquemont (Würtemberg)	34	4	7	= 25,000
VI Corps Marmont	Bouet (French) . . . / Compans ,, . . . / Frederich ,, . . .	39	4	20	= 22,000

	Divisions.	Batts.	Squdrns.	Batteries.	Men·
XI Corps	Gérard } French and / Fressinet } Italian / Charpentier } mixed	31	2	8	= 17,000
XII Corps	Lorencez (French) . . / Pachtod ,, . . / Raglovich (Bavarian) .	33	0	7	= 24,000
Guards	Old Guard . . . / 2 Divisions Young Guards / Dumoustier and Barrois	6 / 25–30	— / —	— / 14	= 4,000 / = 15,000
Guard Cavalry		—	20	3	= 4,000
1st Cav. Corps Latour Maubourg	Bruyère— / 8 French Regiments = 12,000 men / 1 Regiment Italian } / Chasseurs } 2,400 / 2 Regts. Saxons } / Division Chatel— / 1,800 French detached to V Corps . . / Division Heavy Cavalry . / Division Bourdesoulles— / 6 French Regts., 1,200 / 2 Saxon Regts., 1,200 / Division Doumerc— / 6 French Regts. 1,200 / 1 Neapolitan Regt.1,000	—	45–50	4	= 9,800
				Total . . .	115,000

ARMY UNDER MARSHAL NEY.

	Divisions	Batts.	Squdrns.	Batteries.	Men.
III Corps Ney	Souham . . . . . / Delmas . . . . . / Albert . . . . . / Ricard	66	8	12	= 30,000
V Corps Lauriston	Maisons } / Lagrange } French . / Rochambeau } / Puthod (mixed . . .	30 / 14	— / —	10 / 2	= 19,000 / = 8,000
VII Corps Reynier	Durutte (French). . . / Sohr (Saxon)	16	1	2	= 9,500
II Corps Victor	1st and 4th French Divisions	22	—	2	= 13,000
Châtel's Division of Light Cavalry detached from 1st Cavalry Corps to march with V Corps, 1,800 men .		—	9	—	= 1,800
II Cavalry Corps. Sebastiani . .		—	15	—	= 3,000
				Total . . .	84,000

123

The two Armies together totalled 200,000 men, but were evidently a very heterogeneous collection, particularly weak in Cavalry, and guns for all the Batteries were not complete, so that the proportion was barely 2 instead of the normal 3 per thousand bayonets, but the Allies had received far fewer reinforcements, and on the morning of the battle of Bautzen could not dispose of more than 110,000 over the whole theatre of operations, of which only 90,000 could by any possibility take part in the fighting.

Simultaneously, whilst re-organizing the Army, the Emperor's attention was directed to the preparation of Dresden as a base of operations.

Three bridges were completed with their approaches and defences, and hospitals, magazines, etc., were all prepared; that is to say, orders were given to that effect, but subsequent events make it doubtful whether they were all obeyed.

The following *routes de l'Armée* were decreed:

1st.	Main road from Mainz to Dresden, by Frankfurt, Fulda, Erfurt, Weimar; with two branches, one by Jena to Altenburg; the other by Naumburg and Leipzig
2nd.	A branch from Leipzig to Wittenberg
3rd.	A branch from Augsburg to Altenburg by Nuremberg, Bamberg Schleiz and Gera

The Augsburg-Würzburg road was suppressed. Halting-places were arranged every six leagues (18 miles) and troops moving along the roads were given one day's rest for six to seven day's marching.

As Col. Lanrezac, whose account I am here following almost textually, points out, the suppression of the links from Erfurt to Dresden *via* Altenburg and of the Würzburg road was not altogether wise, for partisans continually interfered with the Leipzig line, and orders had to be issued that detachments should march in bodies not less than 500 strong, with all due military precautions.

The main road from Dresden to Bautzen runs across the

many forest-clad spurs which descend from the crest of the Riesengebirge. The country was sparsely cultivated and always inhospitable, whilst every day's delay gained by the resistance of their rear guards was employed by the Allies to drive off cattle and forage. The fact that the two Armies, after passing the Elbe, had utilized every available road, and covered their retreat with Cossacks, made it very difficult for Napoleon to decide on the true direction they had adopted. The troops that had gone north to Groszenhayn might very well have been sent to join Büllow before Berlin, hence the Emperor hesitated before making a final decision, and on May 13, he wrote a letter to Ney, which shows clearly what was in his mind.

> I cannot yet see clearly what the Prussians are doing; it is certain that the Russians are retreating on Breslau; but the Prussians—are they also retiring to that town, or have they thrown themselves on Berlin, *as seems natural, to defend their capital?* The reports I expect tonight will clear the matter up. You will understand that with the considerable forces at your disposal there can be no question of sitting down with folded hands. To relieve Glogau, to occupy Berlin, so that the Prince d'Eckmühl (Davoût) can re-occupy Hamburg, and advance with his five Divisions (he had only three) through Pomerania to seize Berlin, these are the three objects I propose to attain during the month. By the position I have assigned to you, we shall always be able to concentrate and move either to the right or left according to circumstances.

According to the orders already sent to him, Ney would occupy on May 16, with the III Corps and his own Headquarters, Luckau, with the V Corps Dobrilugh, VII Corps Dahme and the II Corps with 2nd Cavalry Corps, Schönwald. The centre of this group is about seventy miles from Dresden. Bautzen is thirty-five miles from Dresden, and about sixty from Luckau; and in view of the fact that the Allies in their own country were always well informed of the French movements, the temptation to move behind the screen of forest land to deliver a stroke on Ney with the whole united Army, must have been great for the Prussians, for they at least could change their base from Silesia to Berlin. But Napoleon gauged the consequences of the Alliance correctly, and though he certainly expected that the latter would try to cover their capital (in which case Ney could easily hold them till he arrived in person) he was convinced that the conflicting interests of the two parties could never be reconciled sufficiently to admit of concerted action.

Meanwhile, as we have already seen, the IV, VI, and XI Corps had crossed the Elbe on the 11th, and on the same day Macdonald's Corps (XI) overtook the Russian rear guard under Miloradowitch at Weissig, on the road to Stolpen, and a sharp action resulted. The Russians withdrew as night came on, and took post at Bischofswerda, where they were again attacked by Macdonald. The fighting on this day was very serious; the village itself was burnt to the ground, and though the Russians again retreated, morning found them only a few miles east of the position they had abandoned, and quite ready to renew the action. For the next two days the French remained watching them whilst the IV Corps (Bertrand) moved by the main road towards Bautzen as far as Königsbrück, encountering only Cossacks, the VI Corps (Marmont), following in second line to Reichenburg.

Supplies, however, immediately began to create difficulties, and the complaints of the Marshals against the barbarous methods of the enemy in clearing the country read quaintly from the very men who had first set the example of making "war support war" under other conditions.

The Cossacks, backed by Prussian Light Cavalry, also began to make themselves troublesome, and on the 12th, detachments reached the Elbe near Meissen from Groszenhayn necessitating the dispatch of Latour Maubourg's Cavalry and a supporting force of Infantry to keep communication open with Ney.

The degree of insecurity produced by these raids is indicated by the fact that all important dispatches were now sent off in triplicate, and were frequently entrusted to friendly Saxons in disguise, whilst all provisions had to be sent up to the front in convoy under escort. In six days *nearly one-third of the Cavalry horses* were broken down from want of forage.

By midnight on the 13th, all doubts as to the direction of the Prussian retreat were set at rest by the comparison of the reconnaissance reports sent in during the previous forty-eight hours, but whether the two armies now reunited at Bautzen would stand their ground or retreat further to Breslau required to be cleared up.

With this object, the following orders 14th May were issued at 4 a m. on the 14th.

The XI Corps remains in position at Bischofswerda.

The IV Corps by Kamenz, advance guard to Kloster Marienstern on the way to Bautzen.

The VI Corps closes up to Frankenthal (three miles west of Bischofswerda).

The XII Corps by Weissig to Fischbach.

Imperial Guard to remain in and around Dresden.

On the 15th, Macdonald (XI) resuming his advance beyond Bischofswerda encountered the Russian rear guard at Göda, and after hard fighting drove it back till he came within sight of Bautzen, and the camps of the Allies about that place.

To the north the IV Corps also came within touch of the enemy about Bautzen and established communication with Macdonald on its right. The VI and XII also closed up in support.

It now seemed clear that the enemy intended to receive battle, for numerous entrenchments were observed on the heights above Bautzen, and the inhabitants reported the arrival of reinforcements to join the Allied Forces.

In order to complete the defeat of the Allies at Bautzen, it was Napoleon's intention to send Ney with his III Corps to join the troops already assembled there. Berthier was directed to inform Ney in due course, but by some misunderstanding he failed to make it clear to Ney that the order issued by the Emperor's command was merely a "Corps", and not an "Army" order. Berthier had forgotten that Ney was in command of the whole force, as well as his own special Corps (III). Very naturally, when Ney received his order to advance, knowing the importance of the coming engagement, he took with him on the 17th 85,000 men, including Victor with the II and VII Corps. The Emperor had intended on the 14th to send definite orders to Victor to advance from Lückau towards Berlin, but the matter was somehow overlooked, and only on the 18th was the omission rectified; an illuminating instance of Staff management in the Grand Army as it was. Such an oversight would be inconceivable in a continental Staff nowadays.

Meanwhile, twenty-four hours later, the Emperor changed his mind again, and Ney received an order to take Victor and the VII Corps with him (II Corps understood, as that was Victor's special command). Now Victor had already marched with Ney, but Ney having started in a single column his 85,000 men were strung out over thirty miles of highway. Had Napoleon been marching to fight, in order to get his men up as quickly as possible, and as nearly as might be close together, he would have marched them in masses of Divisions, with only the guns on the roads. Under these conditions he would have had his troops up to the point whence they could deploy into the fighting lines in far less time, and with less confusion, than men marching in column could have been handled. Victor with his 35,000 being in rear of Ney's troops could not get past to obey the Emperor's order as sent to him, and failed in consequence to reach the battlefield until after the Allies had made good their retreat from the field of Bautzen.

On the morning of the 18th, Ney's troops occupied the following positions:

V Corps (3 Divisions)	at Leutenberg
III Corps and Headquarters	at Kahlau
VII Corps and Headquarters	at Lückau
II Corps & 2nd Cavalry Corps	at Dahme

On the same day the Emperor left Dresden with the Guards for Harthau, half way to Bautzen, and before starting wrote the accompanying letter for Berthier (the "Major-General", as he was always called).

Dresden
4 a.m., 18th May
Send orders to the Duc de Treviso (Mortier) and to General Latour Maubourg, to move tomorrow to Bischofswerda.

As soon as the head of his column arrives, the Duc de Reggio (Oudinot) will deploy into line of battle. Re-iterate the order to him to occupy Neukirch, and the positions on the right, so as to make sure that no enemy remains in those forests.

Send orders also to General Latour Maubourg to search out all the country to the right and actively pursue any Cossacks he may find on the roads from Neustadt to Neukirch.

Order the Old Guard with the reserves of Artillery to start from 4 to 8 a.m., and make a day's march on the Bautzen road.

Give orders to Barrois' Division (Young Guard) to hold itself ready to move off at 11 a.m. I think it will be nec-essary to distribute a pound of rice to each soldier of the Old Guard and of Barrois' Division; that will make a reserve for four days in case of a block amongst the transport.

Reiterate the order to General Bertrand (IV Corps) to place himself in communication with General Lauriston (V Corps) and the Prince de la Moskova, who are due today at Königswerda.

I suppose the Field Headquarters have started; send on everything necessary for a day of battle.

I have cited this order as typical; for the total absence of any form, its want of precision, and the way in which points to be attended to are jotted down almost at random, gives one the insight necessary to appreciate the peculiar functions of the "Major-General" in the machinery of the whole Army. It was his duty to comb out and disentangle these ideas, and transmit them with the necessary additions, to their several addresses, and the slightest want of form or courtesy in the final order seems often to have been bitterly resented by the recipients.[1] When in addition to these sources of friction, the uncertainty and irregularity in the arrival of the orders themselves at their destination is taken into consideration, one can only marvel at the high average of success which this almost casual staff service attained. The chief explanation, of course, is *that the whole Army, Emperor and Marshals, were so accustomed to War and its chances that the latter "played the game" on a mere indication from their chief*—but as events will presently show, *that indication was the essential factor in the whole matter.*

We have seen above that mistakes and delay in the receipt of orders had thrown Ney's command twenty-four hours behindhand in the whole combination. On the morning of the 19th his troops resumed their march in accordance with the orders written on the 17th, but received on the evening of May 18, but these were so laconic, and conveyed so little in-

---

1. *Foucart*, p. 258; letter from Oudinot, May 18, 1813.

formation as to the position of the enemy, that Ney misunderstood their purport altogether, and his columns were actually heading for a position in the left rear of the Grand Army, instead, as intended, to the right rear of the enemy.

Fortunately the unexpected action of Allies interfered to prevent this *contretemps*. They had determined to strike a blow at the converging columns outside the zone of their position, and to this end a force of 18,000 men of all arms under Barclay de Tolly and Yorck set out very early in the morning, and news of their approach being given to General Lauriston (V Corps) he closed up his troops for action and brought up their right shoulders to meet them.

This movement left the flank of the IV Corps exposed, and its outermost Division (Peyri's Italians), marching in to Königswartha without proper precaution, was suddenly overwhelmed and severely handled.

The further advance of the V Corps, however, disengaged them, and Yorck and Barclay fell back in the night on their main position. But the unexpected attack completely upset Ney, who now drew up his troops for the night facing east, instead of south, as he had originally intended doing; and in notifying the fight to Napoleon he stated his intention to fall back on Buchwald if the attack were renewed in the morning. In that event, he begged that support should be sent him from the IV Corps on his right. Nothing could serve better to show how completely Ney misunderstood his own rôle, and the whole conception underlying the Napoleonic system; but fortunately further orders to continue his march via Klix reached him in sufficient time to avert misfortune.

The Emperor in the meanwhile had reached the Grand Army in front of Bautzen and had reconnoitred the enemy's]position as far as it was visible. During the afternoon of the 19th the positions of the several Corps of the Grand Army were corrected for the battle expected on the following day.

The enemy held the line of the Spree with strong out-posts, and as before said many entrenchments were visible on the heights to the westward. Bautzen itself, with its me-diaeval ramparts, was strongly held, and north of the village or townlet a succession of inundations and ponds rendered access to the position beyond somewhat difficult. South of the town the stream rapidly decreased in depth as it neared its sources in the main-chain of the Bohemian frontier; on the other hand its banks became steep and in some plac-es precipitous, whilst numerous patches of forest rendered concealment easy on either side.

Recognizing that such ground suited to perfection the tactics which all Europe had come to consider the especial characteristic of the French Infantry, the Allies from the first regarded this wing, *i.e.* their left, as the most exposed to at-tack, and feeling its weakness, had prepared a second position about three miles in rear of the Spree, indicated by the line of the Blossauer Wasser, a small affluent of the Spree, where more open ground on their own side gave greater facility of manœuvre, particularly for their Cavalry, which formed their main strength. The right wing of the Allies rested on a group of small *kopjes* about two miles north-east of Bautzen, and throughout the position villages had been fortified, and redoubts and batteries erected.

Wittgenstein, who still officiated as Commander-in-Chief, had determined to fight a defensive-offensive battle within his prepared position—and his voluminous orders provided for every possible contingency, *except the one that arose.* The extreme front of the position was about 15,000 yards, alto-gether too great for the 85,000 men, which seems an outside estimate of the numbers actually available for its defence.

Owing to the various *contretemps* which had arisen in Ney's command, the Emperor had a difficult problem to adjust. Bar-clay's reconnaissance in force of the previous day must have completely enlightened the Allies as to their danger if they continued to hold their ground. On the other hand, a direct assault on their carefully prepared position could only be attended with very heavy sacrifice, and the Emperor was in no position to throw away men for anything but the prospect of an adequate return.

Remembering his previous experience of Russian methods, he could not overlook the very great possibility of their retreat during the night if he neglected to hold them during the day. His only chance, therefore, of holding them lay in involving them in such a severe fight that it would be difficult for them to break it off and retire under cover of darkness. With this object the morning of the 20th was spent in ostentatious movements of the centre of the Army—which in itself was not numerically imposing enough to frighten the enemy off his ground, whilst they on the extreme left and Oudinot on the right moved into their positions under cover.

About 4 p.m. he put his troops in motion, and whilst sending Oudinot (XII Corps) against his enemy's left, he advanced the remainder of his Army down to the river, and under cover of a tremendous cannonade threw trestle bridges across the stream and drove in all the enemy's outposts.

So far this was exactly what the Allies wanted. Their hope had been throughout to induce the French to cross over to their side of the Spree, and then to attack out of their prepared and concealed position on the Blossauer Wasser. They had also succeeded in rather more than holding their own against Oudinot's attack on their left, and no sign of danger from Ney's troops on the north had as yet become apparent. They, therefore, reinforced their left and determined to continue the battle next day.

This was what Napoleon had anticipated and as the arrival of Ney on their right was now certain, he fully expected a victory on the grandest scale. Making every allowance for possible delays *en route,* he ordered Ney to continue his movement via Klix on Preititz, a position well in rear of the enemy's right, and to be there at 11 a.m. Then between 11 a.m. and noon, the general attack would be delivered along the whole line. Meanwhile, Oudinot, reinforced by part of the XI Corps, was to advance against the enemy's left at daybreak, and push the attack home. The centre of the Army was to stand fast until the Emperor gave the word.

Thus the battle began with renewed fury on the Allied left, and the Royal Headquarters rode out to a little knoll near Baschütz, from whence they overlooked the whole of Napoleon's centre, and could watch the progress of the struggle on their left. Their view to the right (north-west) appears to have been interrupted by the ground, in any case their attention was completely absorbed by the scene in front of them. For very soon the French attack began to be held, and presently it was clear that the Russians were making headway, in the excitement of the moment, reports from Barclay on their right appear to have been neglected, at any rate no sufficient attention was paid to them. Here Ney was driving everything before him with overwhelming numbers, and away beyond his left, heavy masses of troops, the V Corps, were showing.

By 10 a.m. Ney had reached Preititz, but his orders told him to be there at 11 a.m. Unfortunately a roll of the ground hid him from Napoleon, who had ridden forward to a low *kopje* near, and being left without guidance Ney concluded to wait until the appointed time for his appearance. This delay saved the Allies, for now their danger became apparent to them and orders were issued to retreat, but the troops actually in contact with the enemy were to resist as long as was practicable.

The consequent slackening of resistance along the centre did not escape Napoleon, who in the interval had brought up the Guards for the decisive blow, and about 3 p.m. he gave the signal for the final advance. Meanwhile Ney had become absorbed in the fight raging to his right front, and entirely forgetting his instructions to continue his march from

Preititz on Weissenburg, a point well on the line of retreat of the Allies, he made his troops bring up their left shoulders and advanced almost southwest across the field. Three French Corps converged on the plateau—just as the Prussians who had hitherto held it had received orders to retreat. As the several French columns rose above the slopes they found themselves face to face with one another. The jaws of the trap had closed, but they held nothing between them, for the Prussians had vanished unseen. These incidents are not infrequent on manœuvre grounds, and take some time even then to straighten out. In the confusion incident to the close range fighting of a century ago. the scene which ensued can be imagined, not described.

This was the opportunity of the Allies, and they seized it. Covered by their excellent Cavalry they withdrew in order, and with all possible rapidity, and by nightfall were far on their way towards Görlitz, leaving for the second time not a single trophy to grace the conqueror's victory.

Situated politically as Napoleon was, this second failure to reap the rewards of a crushing success was almost as disastrous as an actual defeat. With 200,000 men at his disposal—170,000 of whom had actually appeared upon the field, he had failed to capture a single gun or stand of colours. The Allies with less than half his force had resisted all his efforts to beat them for two whole days, and though the reason of this resistance was clear enough to him, he could hardly explain the fact away without seriously damaging the prestige of his Army and its Commanders. His one chance of retrieving the situation lay in a rapid and relentless pursuit, which he immediately initiated. But the heart was out of his Army. His men had not seen their enemy beaten. The failure of the last great blow which should have shattered the *"moral"* of the Allies beyond retrieval, and turned them from a fighting Army into a frightened flock of sheep, exalting the courage of the victors in proportion as the panic reaction spread through the flying masses, had robbed the French troops of the chief stimulus for further exertion, and they stumbled on blindly, too weary to guard themselves efficiently against possible attack. Each day of the pursuit brought fresh and bitter experience. On May 22, finding the enemy in position just beyond Reichenberg, instead of *dashing* at them with the old confidence and *élan,* they halted to manœuvre them out of position, and Napoleon galloping up at the moment, impatient at the way his men were checking, sent forward Latour Maubourg's Cavalry who were suddenly ambushed by a couple of Russian Horse Artillery batteries, and before they could recover from the surprise, they were charged and very roughly handled[1] by the Allied cavalry. The sudden engagement had to take its course, and after a stubborn fight the Russian rear guard, having gained all possible time, began its retirement. Reynier, whose Corps (VII) had been making forced marches four days running, now begged for authority to halt and rest his men. But Napoleon only ordered him forward, though he had yielded to a similar appeal less well founded, after the battle of Eckmühl in 1809. A few moments later a spent cannon ball struck down Marshal Duroc, his most faithful and devoted friend. The shock upset even the Emperor's iron nerve; he was profoundly affected, and ordered the firing to cease. That night the Allies bivouacked about Görlitz.

On the 23rd, the pursuit was continued, and on the following days also. Each time the Emperor demanded another 20 miles, which the troops were too worn out to accomplish.

On the side of the Allies the outlook was also far from promising. They had lost on the battlefield about 20,000 men, and what was worse, all confidence in each other and in their leader had departed. Wittgenstein's position had become impossible. He offered his resignation, which was accepted, and Barclay de Tolly was appointed to the chief command in his

---

1. Their losses, however, were only reported at 100 men.

place. But this scarcely mended matters. Barclay, of Scots extraction, as his name sufficiently indicates, took a very cool and level-headed view of the situation, and refused altogether to satisfy the patriotic but impracticable longings of the Prussians for another battle. The troops were far too spent for there to be any prospect of success were they allowed to fight, and a thorough reorganization was essential, but when the opportunity for that might arrive remained very doubtful.

On May 26, the Prussian Cavalry, under Blücher, prepared an ambush for the V Corps, which formed the advance guard of the French Left Column. It had been observed marching without adequate precaution, and Maison's Division, which led the march, was ridden into and dispersed. Then the French grew more cautious, but Napoleon had already reopened negotiations begun after Lützen for an armistice on the basis of *uti possidetis.* He, therefore, felt it necessary to press on and occupy Breslau. After leaving the line of the Katzbach at Leignitz and Goldberg, the Allies had bent away to the south-east, by Jauer on Schweidnitz, leaving the road to Breslau open, and in the course of June 1, the French entered that town, whilst the Allies concentrated on Schweidnitz. The indomitable energy of the Emperor had again triumphed over all obstacles, and if the Allies stood their ground, as in fact they had resolved to do, it would seem, from the map, that their doom was certain. The French stood on a front of 30 miles from Jauer to Breslau, and in thirty-six hours must have penned them against the Austrian frontier.

It was probably this fact which induced the Emperor finally to agree to the Armistice, a step in his career which has received more unfavourable criticism than any other. That, I take it, is because enthusiasm for the "Art of the Leader", *i.e.* strategy, has blinded the critics to the essential fact that strategy is after all only the servant of National Policy, and policy rendered the step inevitable, as will now be demonstrated. Theoretically Austria was still the Ally of France. Practically the Emperor already knew that she meant to betray him; for months her conduct had been more than suspect, and it was clear that the large Army he knew she was concentrating in Bohemia was not intended to aid his (Napoleon's) designs. If the Allies stood to receive battle, he had not men enough to surround them, and defeat would only have precipitated a hostile declaration from Austria. If the Allies retreated yet further, the danger of the presence of this Austrian Army on the flank of his long unguarded line of communications would become greater with every march in pursuit.

Want of Cavalry was the principal military reason which Napoleon put forward in explanation of his consent to an Armistice, and his German critics, notably Graf Yorck von Wartenburg, have always maintained that this reason was insufficient to justify his conduct. This, however, I submit, is because they have systematically viewed this Cavalry question from the standpoint of its reconnoitring value, and not from that of its "victory completing" power.

Situated as he now was, it must have been quite clear to the Emperor, after the experiences of Lützen and Bautzen, that he could no longer hope to win a really decisive battle, such as would of itself bring the War to a close. His Artillery might tear out gaps in the enemy's line with case fire, but in face of the enemy's superior Cavalry, his Infantry could only avail themselves of the lanes of death thus formed by marching in dense columns, ready to form square at a moment's notice. This, he knew, meant delay, which the enemy utilized to break off the fighting. If he could afford to wait for six weeks he could make good this deficiency in the proportion of the Cavalry arm. It would also enable him, not only to fill up the gaps in the existing Corps, due to battle and sickness (principally to the latter—there were 90,000 sick on the morning states of the first week in June), but he could place new Corps now in process of formation in his fighting line, and thus bring up his available field forces to a figure that the

Allies, even with Austria included, could hardly hope to exceed. If then, Napoleon could once involve the whole Army of the Allies in a single decisive battle, he had every reason for expecting to end the War by a single blow, for his superiority as a Leader rose relatively to the command on the side of his enemies, almost in proportion to the numbers to be controlled. In other words, he, with his Marshals under his own eye, on one battlefield with 200,000 might safely be trusted to make fewer mistakes than would his opponents at the head of an equal number, and the greater the numbers to be handled, the better his chances of necessity became.

Actually the conduct of operations by his adversaries, as we shall presently see, never gave him his hoped-for opportunity, but at the time it was impossible for him to forecast this.

To make the picture of the Emperor's situation complete, it must be remembered that he had left Dresden with only ammunition enough for *"un jour de bataille,"* and his march had been so rapid that his trains could not overtake the troops; and further that Oudinot (the Duke of Reggio), who had been detached after Bautzen to cover the French rear from the direction of Berlin, was facing Büllow near Luckau, and was in fact, badly beaten by him on June 9, before the news of the Armistice could reach either side. Further Tschernitschew's Cossacks had dispersed a regiment of provisional Cavalry on May 25, near Halle, and had captured on the 30th a convoy of Artillery and its escort of 1,600 men near Halberstadt. In addition to this Woronzow, who had been left behind to observe Magdeburg, had made a descent on Leipzig, and was actually driving the French garrison out of its gates when news of the Armistice, arriving very opportunely, put a stop to the fighting. The two most important of these incidents happened after the Armistice, it is true, but they suffice to show how very real were the dangers to which the French lines of communication were exposed.

CHAPTER 6

The Armistice

The foundations of the new Grand Army were laid, as we
have already seen, by Napoleon's Decree of the 12th March.
All the Corps therein provided for could not be made ready
for the field in time to take part in the operations beyond
Dresden in May, but an enormous number of conscripts were
already on the march before the Armistice, principally belonging to the levy of 1813, but embodying also many recal-
citrants *(réfractaires)*[1] of previous years, and these sufficed to fill
the ranks of all the existing Corps, at the front, as well as to
complete the I, II, XII, III, and XIV Corps, whose formation
had scarcely been begun when their Headquarters were hurried up to the front. The Cavalry Corps were also brought up
to full strength or nearly so; hence at the close of the Armistice the French Army stood in the following order[2]:

---

1. *Les Réfractaires* was the name given to the peculiarly recalcitrant deserters, who had to be hunted down by flying columns of troops like brigands.
When a sufficient number had been caught, every tenth man was shot on
a public parade and the remainder sent off to the Isles of Oleron and Rhé
or similar places, where they were placed under officers selected for their
tact and comprehension of men, and once they understood that escape was
impossible, they accepted their fate and often made excellent soldiers. They
used to be sent by companies along the coast to Holland, and from thence
were marched to the front, so as not to expose them to the temptation of
desertion in their own country. They may fairly be compared to the men we
«pressed» into the Navy, but were undoubtedly treated with greater humanity.
2. From *Friedrich,* vol. I, p. 62.

		Battalions.	Squadrons.	Guns.	Men.
The Guards .		62	59	218	= 58,191
I Corps.	Vandamme .	42	4	76	= 33,298
II ,,	Victor .	43	6	76	= 25,158
III ,,	Ney .	62	11	122	= 40,006
IV ,,	Bertrand	36	8	72	= 23,663
V ,,	Lauriston	37	7	74	= 27,905
VI ,,	Marmont	42	8	84	= 27,754
VII ,,	Reynier .	33¼	13	68	= 21,283
VIII ,,	Poniatowski [2] (Poles) .	10	6	44	= 7,573
XI ,,	Macdonald .	38	7	90	= 24,418
XII ,,	Oudinot .	30	14	58	= 19,324
XIII ,,	Davoût	47	15	76	= 37,514
XIV ,,	St. Cyr (Gouvion) .	51	12	92	= 26,411
					372,236

CAVALRY CORPS

			Guns.	Men.
1st Cavalry Corps.	Latour Maubourg .	78	36	= 16,537
2nd ,, ,,	Sebastiani .	52	18	= 10,304
3rd ,, ,,	Arighi .	27	24	= 6,000
4th ,, ,,	Kellermann	24	12	= 3,923
5th ,, ,,	L'Héritier .	20	6	= 4,000
				40,764

	Battalions.	Squadrons.	Guns.	Men.
Girard's Corps .	10	16	28	= 15,000
Artillery and Engineers, Reserve Park .	—	—	—	= 8,010
Corps of Observation at Leipzig. General Margaron .	10	8	10	= 7,800

Grand total of Field Troops—559¼ battalions, 395 squadrons, 1,284 guns = 442,810 men.

In the above list the numbers IX and X are omitted; the former was reserved for the Bavarian Corps (Wrede) and was subsequently transferred to the Corps of Augereau, still in process of formation, and the latter under Rapp formed the garrison of Danzig.

Poniatowski's Corps had been shut up in Warsaw during the first half of the campaign, but was allowed free passage by the Allies, as their presence in rear of the front detained more men for their supervision than they were considered to be worth.

GARRISON OF FORTRESSES ON THE ELBE,
EXCLUSIVE OF FIELD TROOPS IN THE COMMAND.

Hamburg .	12,000
Bremen .	1,500
Magdeburg .	3,250
Wittenberg .	2,318
Torgau .	2,000
Dresden .	5,000
Total on the Elbe .	26,068

SECOND LINE TROOPS.

Lemoine's Division at Minden	5,400
Augereau's Corps, about	10,000
Cavalry Corps Milhaud, in formation . . .	2,500
Bavarian Corps, Wrede	25,000
	42,900

GARRISONS OF FORTRESSES IN POLAND AND GERMANY.

Danzig	25,000
Zamoscz	4,000
Modlin	3,000
Stettin	8,500
Küstrin	4,000
Glogau	5,500
Erfurt	1,874
Würzburg	2,500
	55,374

Add to all these reinforcements on their way to the frontier, sick and wounded in hospital, troops of the Bavarian and Westphalian contingents, not included in the above, and the grand total of all cannot well fall short of 700,000, available more or less within the German theatre of operations.

On the whole the average quality of the troops must be considered as somewhat better than those that fought at Lützen, even though the age of the conscripts who had filled up the gaps in the field Army was fractionally lower. The troops had fully recovered their confidence in the Emperor; the weakest elements in *moral* and physique alike had been eliminated and the remaining cadres of old war-seasoned non-commissioned officer's and men readily absorbed their contingent of recruits, and imbued them with their own rigorously trained spirit. It must be remembered that no man reached the ranks with less than ninety days' training, sixty of which at least had been spent on the line of march, and the physically weak had been removed by the process of the survival of the fittest.

The Cavalry, however, were still the weakest point in Napoleon's organization. They were, as a whole, miserably mounted on horses not broken but broken down, though they possessed some leaders of the highest, quality, who knew

142

their men and their work (de Brac; for instance) and their exploits at Dresden and Leipzig prove that under competent commanders they were still capable of efficient service.

The Artillery was always excellent, and in spite of deficient horse supply showed a uniform superiority over that of the Allies.

The greatest advantage that the French possessed over the Allies lay not alone in the incontestable superiority of the Emperor himself, whether as strategist or tactician, but in the uniform war experience of the Marshals, their Divisional Commanders, Staff and subaltern officers.

The condition of the Allied troops when for the time hostilities ceased was little if at all better than that of their opponents. Battalions had shrunk, in some cases to 200 men and even less, and the survivors were spent with the constant strain of marching and fighting. But the Prussians at least were in the heart of their own country, and knew that they were fighting for very existence. The Russians on the whole were older men, of longer service, and far more accustomed to hardship and privation. The men had forgotten, if indeed they had ever known, any other tie but that of the Regiment, and as long as that held together they were at home in the only "home" they were capable of realizing. Moreover, they recovered from the depression due to their heavy, almost daily, losses with the fatalism peculiar to their race.

The losses of the Prussian field troops were made good by recruits with an average of about three months under arms; and since all were filled with the same spirit of goodwill for the service and a fierce desire to close with the enemy, these new drafts were soon assimilated by the war-seasoned ranks of the older men.

By the end of July, the *Landwehr* also were sufficiently ready for the field. Under normal circumstances they would certainly not have passed the easiest of reviewing officers, for in many cases the front rank was armed only with pikes, their clothing was anything but regulation, and their foot gear beneath contempt. But events proved, as they so often have done before and since, that a regulation equipment is not absolutely essential for men who really wish to conquer their enemies, therefore once these rough troops had become accustomed to their new surroundings, they did excellent service. In all they made up 37 Regiments in 149 Battalions (Friedrich, II, 43), averaging about 680 men; so that we may count them in round numbers as 100,000.

The Cavalry of the Landwehr seems to have been on the whole markedly better than its Infantry, but according to the Cavalry officers of the old Army, they were quite deplorable. They were always willing to charge, but the difficulty was to rally them, and Marwitz, in his diary has many anecdotes about them.[1] But the spirit was in them, and they were about as good as the bulk of their opponents. Altogether they supplied 116 squadrons of a total strength of about 10,000 men. Adding Artillery and Engineers, the grand total of armed men available amounted to about 275,000, to which some 25,000 reinforcements joined during the campaign, must be added.[2]

These numbers were organized in the following manner (Friedrich, II, 47):

FIELD ARMY.

	Battalions.	Squadrons.	Guns.		Men.
(a) In Silesia—					
The Guards	6½	8	16	=	7,091
I Corps. Yorck	45	44	104	=	38,484
II „ Kleist	41	44	112	=	37,816
(b) In Brandenburg—					
III Corps. Bülow	40½	42	80	=	41,135
IV „ Tauentzien	48½	29	42	=	33,170
The Partisans of Lützow, Reiche and					
Schill	4	7	8	=	4,068
	185½	174	362	=	161,764

1. See Cavalry Past and Future.
2. 300,000 men out of a population of 5,000,000 is about 6 per cent. 6 per cent, of our total population gives about 2,500,000, but as a fact we have over 3,000,000 trained to arms between the ages of eighteen and sixty.

		Battalions.	Squadrons.	Guns.	Men.
For Blockade of Küstrin		9	5	8 =	7,122
„ „ Stettin		15	7	8 =	10,548
„ „ Danzig		10	6	8 =	8,000
„ „ Glogau		9	4	16 =	5,000
		43	22	40 =	30,670

Grand total of troops actually organized : 228½ battalions, 196 squadrons, 402 guns= 192,434 men.

Russian Army The total number of Russian troops on German territory at the conclusion of the Armistice amounted to 296,000 men, grouped as follows :—

(a) In Silesia—

	Battalions.	Squadrons.	Cossack Regts.	Guns.	Men.
Langeron's Corps . . .	47	15	10	139 =	34,551
Sacken's „ . . .	18	30	12	60 =	18,553
Wittgenstein's Corps . .	45	38	5	92 =	34,926
St. Priest's Corps . . .	20	22	3	36 =	13,586
Guards and Reserves, under the Grand Duke Constantine	47	71	10	182 =	44,347
	177	176	40	509 =	145,763

(b) In Brandenburg—

	Battalions.	Squadrons.	Cossack Regts.	Guns.	Men.
Winzengerode					
Woronzow	29	44	20	92 =	29,357
Tschernitschew . . .					
Attached to Bülow's Corps	—	—	3	22 =	1,160
Attached to Tauentzien's Corps	—	—	1	— =	318
	29	44	24	114 =	30,835

(c) In Mecklenburg, attached to Walmoden's Corps—

	Battalions.	Squadrons.	Cossack Regts.	Guns.	Men.
Detachment Tettenborn .	—	—	4	— =	1,495
Russo-German Legion . .	6	—	—	—	4,475
With Dornberg's Cavalry Division	—	8	—	— =	1,192
Russo - German Artillery Brigade	—	—	—	16 =	363
					6,525

Giving a total for the Field Army of 212 battalions, 228 squadrons, 61 Cossack regiments, 639 guns = 184,123 men.

IN SECOND LINE.

About Warsaw—	Battalions.	Squadrons.	Cossack Regts.	Guns.	Men.
Polish Army of Observation under Benningsen . . .	70	67	10	198 =	59,000
Blockading Zamoscz . . .	21	5	3	36 =	15,000
Blockading Modlin	?	?	?	? =	9,000
Siege of Danzig	58	12	11	59 =	29,100
					112,100

The successive campaigns of Austerlitz and Wagram had reduced Austrian finance to a condition of almost hopeless destitution. As a measure of economy, the effectives of the troops had been reduced to the lowest possible point, and, worst of all, the greater part of the workpeople in all the arsenals and Government factories had been discharged. Hence the efforts to raise new forces in 1813 were most severely hampered. Men existed in abundance, but it was difficult to arm and equip them, and the motive of self-preservation not being so overwhelming as in the cane of Prussia, the Generals were by no means so ready to take the field without adequate equipment.

In the middle of the month of August the field states gave the following totals:

In Bohemia : 107 battalions, 117 squadrons, 280 guns,
   under F.M. Prince Schwarzenberg . . . . = 127,345
Between the Ems and Traun, under F.M. Prince Reusz . 30,070
In the interior of Austria, under F.Z.M. Hiller . . . 35,557

                                 192,992
Garrison troops   27,544

          Grand total   221,525

Two-thirds of this force consisted of recruits of three months' service, with little enthusiasm for their work, as until a few days before the expiration of the Armistice they did not know against whom they were to fight. As soon as they found out that the French were to play the rôle of their enemy, the whole Army gained courage and enthusiasm. The Cavalry seems to have been considered the most efficient of all the Allied troops, and the Artillery was fairly good. The Infantry, on the other hand, were below the standard of the other Armies; they had neither the dogged pertinacity of the Russians nor the intense patriotism of the Prussians.[1]

---

1. It is curious to note, taking the statistics of losses in battle by troops of different Nations, over a long period of time, that the Russians have always stood up to a heavier percentage of punishment before breaking up than any other troops on the Continent; the Prussians stand next, the Italians last. The French and Austrians are not easy to analyse; with them everything has turned upon the Man who led them. In the Revolutionary Wars, 2 per cent, seems to have been a fair standard of French endurance; under Napoleon it rose to 28 per cent. The losses in the American Civil War head all the lists.

There remain to be considered—

(a) the Swedish Contingent, amounting in all to 27,263 men. These were excellent material, well found, but the policy of their Commander-in-Chief never gave them a chance of distinguishing themselves;

	Battalions.	Squadrons.	Guns.	Men.
British German Legion . . .	7	—	6 =	4,506
Dornberg's Cavalry Division. .	—	9	— =	1,322
Reserve Artillery of Walmoden's Corps	—	—	12 =	412
The Hanseatic Legions . . .	2	8	8 =	3,043
	9	17	26	9,283

(b) the Anglo-German Contingent—

Note the composition of an "English" battalion—111 Dutchmen, 92 Prussians, 80 Italians, 66 Flemish, 63 Hanoverians and Brunswickers, 46 Frenchmen, 35 Saxons, 27 Austrians, 18 Hamburgers, 14 Bavarians, 14 Hessians, 12 Spaniards, 12 Mecklenburgers, 11 Poles, 10 Holsteiners, 10 Swiss, 9 Hungarians, 7 Danes, 5 Oldenburgers, 3 Russians, 2 Swabians, and 1 Englishman, 1 Portuguese, 1 Swede.

Of these one Hussar regiment of five squadrons, two horse and one rocket battery were nominally British, and six Battalions in British pay formed the garrison of Stralsund.

(c) The Mecklenburg Contingent—

4 battalions, 4 squadrons, 2 guns = 6,149 men.

The sum total of all available Field troops, therefore, amounted to 556½ battalions, 572 squadron 1,380 guns and 68 Cossack regiments = 512,113 men; with, in round figures, 350,000 reserve troops behind them. (Friedrich, vol. I, p. 56 et seq.)

The great difficulty that confronted the Allies at this juncture was to ensure the harmonious co-operation of these very heterogeneous forces, and after much friction the commands were arranged in the following manner.

As the three Sovereigns were to accompany the Army of Bohemia, and as it was assumed that Napoleon would turn first with his full force against Austria, this Army was made very materially the strongest, and the command entrusted to

Field-Marshal Prince Carl von Schwarzenberg. This appointment was severely criticized at the time, for popular feeling was strongly in favour of the Archduke Charles, the victor of Amberg. Würzburg, Stockach, Zürich and Aspern; but political complications with his brother, the Emperor, had rendered him impossible; also he would have been most unpopular with the Russians.

Schwarzenberg, on the other hand, though of no great talent, was peculiarly well fitted to act as conciliator of the many and various interests involved. He was still in the very prime of life, only forty-two; his reputation for personal courage stood very high, and his unselfishness and modesty made it possible to him to adjust the petty jealousies of the war-seasoned veterans around him, as perhaps no other man in Europe at the time could have done. It was no small feather in his cap that in the previous year Napoleon had personally requested his appointment to the command of his Austrian contingent. But he was too humane for War as it had developed during the last few years, and the very strong hint he received before leaving for the front, to the effect that this was the one and only Army that Austria could furnish, was perhaps hardly needed to deter him from adventurous resolves.

His Chief of the Staff, Radetzsky, had seen, if anything, more of War than had even the French Marshals, and seems by universal consent to have been the most able and courageous soldier in the Austrian Army. Unfortunately, however, for the Allies, he was too wanting in personal ambition to assert himself sufficiently; thus it happened that the Quartermaster-General, von Langenau, formerly of the Saxon Army, a brilliant but somewhat unscrupulous man, immeasurably behind Radetzsky in the solid judgment and knowledge of War which characterized the latter, usurped more than his share of the Sovereigns' confidence, with disastrous consequences to the conduct of operations. He was only thirty-two years of age, and owed his reputation chiefly to the fact that he had served for several campaigns under Napoleon, but as events were to prove, he was like Prince Eugene's mule, which, "though it had served in seventeen campaigns under that great General—remained still a mule".

It would probably have been far better for the Allies if they could have agreed to elect any one of the three Sovereigns as Commander-in-Chief; for all of them possessed considerable military talent, and all had acquired the habit of command. But political interests rendered this out of the question, and hence, having no real responsibility, but feeling the necessity of action, they frequently interfered, sometimes indeed most opportunely, but generally with the reverse result, and they always required to be consulted when any question arose as to the employment of their own Guards.

Two renegades attached to the Royal Headquarters deserve a word of mention, *viz.* Moreaü and Jomini. The former had been banished from France in 1804, and had always been considered by his friends as a rival of Napoleon's. However this might be, a cannon shot at Dresden terminated his career before he had an opportunity of establishing this claim. Jomini, a Swiss by birth, had attracted Napoleon's attention in 1805-6 and 1808-9 in Spain. His military writings had given him a European reputation, and as Staff officer to Ney he had certainly rendered valuable service. But he had quarrelled with Berthier, and when, after Bautzen, the latter held him responsible for Ney's many shortcomings, and not without reason one would think, he deserted to the Allies, and was received by the Emperor Alexander. His conduct, however, was so universally deprecated by the officers of all three Armies that (though the Emperor's friend) he was practically boycotted. Disgusted with his reception, he withdrew, after Leipzig, to his native country, and his subsequent writings were markedly tinged with the strong personal bias one would expect from such a character.

For the Silesian Army the choice of the Sovereigns fell on General von Blücher, then in his seventy-first year, and though events have long since justified this selection, at the time it was received by the higher Prussian and Russian officers with almost unqualified disapproval. It was felt that he was far too old, that he was a born gambler, that he drank freely, and was destitute of all knowledge of any other arm but his own—the Cavalry. Of the higher art of War he was considered to know nothing at all; he could not write a decent report, or even spell correctly; he never looked at a map, and the Staff appointed to keep him straight, Gneisenau, Müffling, Rühle von Lilienstern, and Scharnhorst, were all held to be interlopers, or reformers, by the classic old survivors of the Frederickian period, of whom Yorck was the most typical. But Blücher possessed the one great quality of supremest importance in a great emergency of this nature, when men have to be induced to die for their country somehow, *the power of exciting enthusiasm in the Nation, and not merely in the rank and file of the Army.* Yorck, who undoubtedly had higher claims in the Army itself, and who was intellectually and morally immensely Blücher's superior, was his exact antithesis in this latter respect. His conduct at Tauroggen ought to have made him the idol of the Nation, but somehow it failed to do so, and though the men immediately under his command loved him for his care of them and devotion to their interests, it was precisely this attitude of fatherly solicitude for their welfare which would have rendered him useless in supreme Command; he lacked the stern resolution requisite for great emergencies.

Langeron, one of the Russian Corps commanders placed under his orders, resented his supersession even more bitterly than did Yorck himself. He was a French *emigré* who had joined the Russian Army at the beginning of the Revolution, and since then had made a very brilliant career, having held an independent command against the

Turks. He would have hated serving under any foreign officer, but might have submitted with bettor grace to a man of acknowledged military education, and more courtierlike manners than those of rough old Blücher. This feeling of dissatisfaction, which Längeren took no pains to repress, soon spread to the remaining thirty-five generals with which his Corps was overloaded,[1] and throughout the campaign a veiled hostility to Headquarters prevailed, against which the latter were all the more helpless as they did not understand each other's language. Only Sacken seems to have been an exception to this general feeling. He was many years younger than Langeron, of German extraction, and possessed many of the same characteristics as Blücher; in consequence the two understood one another, and Sacken was never called upon in vain.

The Army of the North was given by acclamation to Bernadotte, Crown Prince of Sweden, whose reputation as a Marshal of France stood higher then, before military histories had been written, than it has done since; for as an independent Army Commander he proved an unspeakable failure, as we shall presently see.

The commands having been regulated, it remained to lay down the principles which were to guide the co-operation of these three Armies operating on widely separated lines, and between which inter-communication was, under existing conditions, impossible.

To this end a series of conferences were held, at which endless strategic memoirs were read and discussed. The principal ones are to be found in Friedrich's invaluable work, and deserve attentive study to enable us to get at the spirit of the time. All one can say of them here, is that like the Bourbons, the Staff officers of the period had learnt nothing and forgotten nothing.

---

1. The numerical strength of Langeron's Corps was about 25,000 men.

Since agreement on any one plan was out of the question, a common bond of union was at length found in the universal consensus of opinion that Napoleon himself was the dangerous foe. From this the rest easily followed, and was embodied in a long memorandum known, from the place of its signature, as the agreement of Trachtenberg.

The cardinal principle of this document was that, under no circumstances should any one of the three Armies incur the risk of a decisive action against Napoleon in person. Whichever Army he advanced against was to fall back, whilst the others made the best use of their time and opportunities; and probably no other method could have led to a successful termination of the war.

But it made tremendous demands on the young and untrained troops, burning, in the case of the Prussians at any rate, with patriotic fire, and not yet broken in to understand that the soldier's *highest duty is to die where is he told, not when and where he would like to do so.* Blücher alone proved equal to the situations thus erected, not that he rivalled Napoleon in this greatest gift of a Commander, the psychological power of leading and influencing men, but at least he did more than any other who could have been chosen to fill his position.

Meanwhile, we must return lo Napoleon, who was now busily studying his opening moves for the coming campaign.

His first plan was to arrange for the defence of the whole line of the Elbe, from Königstein in the Bohemian mountains, a little mediaeval fortress perched on a *kopje* overlooking the river, to Hamburg, a line some 400 miles in extent. Across this river he held all the passages, by works, either permanent or provisional, which in the end proved sufficient for his purposes. Throughout the whole district he organized supply depots, and also did something towards the improvement of his lateral communications, though that was singularly little in comparison with what might have been done in the time and with the means at his disposal, considering the importance of such work for the execution of his strategic methods. Road making was as exact a science in those days as it is now, and better roads might have saved him the disaster of Leipzig.

His first idea was a resuscitation of his plan of March 18, *viz.* to mass the bulk of his troops between Magdeburg and Hamburg, and advance on Berlin, seizing the town and thus relieving the garrisons on the Oder. As before calculated, if the Allies came to meet him, he was certain of a decisive battle under most favourable conditions, whilst if they broke forward to the south of Dresden over the Bohemian mountains, he could fall on them in flank and cut them off from all communications. Against this plan was the possibility that they might elect not to stand at all, in which case he would have to follow them into Bohemia, and again exhaust himself by his ever lengthening line of communication. There was always before him *this absolute necessity for the delivery of a decisive battle, as near to the head of his communications as it could be fought.* Ultimately he decided that his best chance of securing such an opportunity would be by taking up a central position with the bulk of his forces between the two principal Armies, those of Silesia and Bohemia, and taking advantage of the first opening which either should offer him. Meanwhile, separate columns, aggregating nearly 120,000 men, should converge on Berlin from Hamburg, Magdeburg, Wittenberg and Bautzen. This latter feature of his plan was so entirely at variance with all his own previous practice, that we can only suppose he adopted it out of complete contempt for the Prussian *Landwehr* in front of him; and more particularly for the military ability of Bernadotte, whose probable conduct of operations he predicted in one of his letters in the following words: *"Il ne fait que piaffer."*

It must be clearly understood that it is the *form* of this movement on Berlin, and not the idea itself, that is here criticized. The threat against his communications contained in the presence of upwards of 100,000 men within about four days' march of the single organized line which connected him with his ultimate base in France, could by no means be overlooked, and no merely passive defence of the 400 miles from Dresden to Hamburg could conceivably be undertaken by those of his forces available for such a purpose. But to place Ney and Davoût under Oudinot, of all men, and to expect the three to execute a combined march of concentration from points several marches apart, seems to have been a voluntary invitation to disaster. As Marmont wrote in reply to a letter written on August 13, 1813, in which Napoleon, after announcing his final decision, asked for his Marshal's free and unfettered opinion of the project—"It is to be feared that on the same day your Majesty wins a great, victory, you will learn that your subordinates have lost two"—a prediction which proved true to the letter.

The decision, however, having been taken, the troops moved rapidly to their appointed position and on August 17 the date on which the Armistice expired, they were in place.

A strong advance guard of four Corps in the square Liegnitz, Goldberg, Lowenberg, Bunzlau. The Main Army under Napoleon, at Görlitz, Zittau, Stolpen and Bautzen. A flanking detachment at Lückau of 60,000 men under Oudinot; whilst the XIV Corp (Gouvion St. Cyr) held the Elbe from Königstein to Dresden, which town Napoleon believed to be sufficiently strong to hold out for at least eight days with the strong garrison assigned to it. *This must be remembered, as it was the keystone of all his arrangements,* which were based on the supposition that the whole Silesian Army was still near Breslau, and the Bohemian Army about Theresienstadt. Viewed from the ordinary standpoint of strategical criticism, the situation appears to the last degree strained and unreal, for the Bohemian Army on the South and Bernadotte on the North already overlap the flanks of the forces immediately opposed to them, both are in a friendly country and therefore presumably well informed as to their enemies' whereabouts, and both are far superior in Cavalry to their immediate opponent. A raid against, or across, Napoleon's communications would therefore seem the obvious plan to adopt, and if strategy really were the "science of communications" as it has sometimes been defined, the extinction of the French Army would seem to be merely a matter of days.

Napoleon was, in fact, quite prepared for the Bohemian Army to make the attempt; indeed the intention to do so had been announced beforehand. When St. Cyr notified the Emperor of the current rumour to this effect, he replied, "If the enemy should march into South Germany, as he proposes, then I shall wish him *'bon voyage'* and let him go, quite certain that he will return quicker than he went. It is only of importance that he should not cut us off from Dresden and the Elbe; I care very little if he severs our communications with France," and he concludes with these remarkable words: "What is certain is that you cannot turn 400,000 men, based on a line of strong places and a river like the Elbe, from which they can break out as they please, either at Dresden, Torgau, Wittenberg or Magdeburg. All the enemy's far-reaching detachments (against French communications understood) will be missing on the day of battle."

The reply to this is of course obvious; *if you cannot turn 400,000 men, etc., you can starve them;* and this is indeed what ultimately happened. But it took two months to do this and had the Emperor's orders been carried out to the letter it would have taken even longer, so ample were the stores and provisions accumulated, on paper. But in two months many battles might be fought, and *a single decisive victory* would have completely transformed the situation.

The truth is *that the value of communications is relative and not absolute, and the Art really consists in knowing when and where it is safe to break the letter of the rules and to provide alternative lines and bases in time to permit change of plans.*

The above distribution was arrived at on the basis of the best information available at the time; but almost on the day the orders were issued, the Allies had made a decision of such magnitude that the Emperor had never taken even its possibility into account On the night of August 11, over 100,000 Russians and Prussian troops broke up from their encampments and set out over the Bohemian mountains to join the Austrians, and some days elapsed before the secret of this sudden movement leaked out.

We have given above the total forces of the several contingents, and such notes as to the personal factors of their commands as are indispensable to the student of military history. It remains now to indicate the final grouping of the forces before the Armistice ran out.

When the above mentioned transfer of Russian and Prussian troops from Silesia to Bohemia was finally effected the order of the Bohemian Army was as follows:—

Commander-in-Chief: F.M. Prince Schwarzenberg.

Chief of Staff: F.M. Lt. Graf. Radetsky.

Quarter Master-General: Major-General Baron Langenau.

1. AUSTRIAN FIELD ARMY.

1st Light Division. Field-Marshal-Lieut. Prince Moritz Liechtenstein. 4 battalions, 12 squadrons, 14 guns= 4,399 men.

2nd Light Division : Field-Marshal-Lieut. Graf. Bubna. 3 battalions, 18 squadrons, 12 guns= 4,400 men.

Right Wing.

Prince von Hessen Homburg.

1st Infantry Division. Field-Marshal-Lieut. Graf. Civalart. 11 battalions, 18 guns= 9,478 men.

2nd Infantry Division. Field-Marshal-Lieut. Graf. Colloredo. 14 battalions, 18 guns= 14,252 men.

1. Infantry Reserve Division (Grenadiers). Field-Marshal-Lieut. Marquis Chasteler. 2 Brigades= 8 battalions, 12 guns, 5,807 men.

2. Infantry Reserve Division. Field-Marshal-Lieut. Bianchi. 3 Brigades= 12 battalions, 13 guns= 10,643 men.

3. Infantry Reserve Division. Field-Marshal-Lieut. Graf. Crenneville. 2 Brigades= 5 battalions, 12 squadrons, 6 guns= 7,004 men.

Cavalry Division. Field-Marshal-Lieut. Graf. Nostitz. (Cuirassiers). 16 squadrons in 2 Brigades, no guns= 2,472 men.

Cavalry Division. Field-Marshal-Lieut. von Schneller. (Light, 21 squadrons in 2 Brigades)= 2,336 men.

Pioneers : 8 companies.

Pontonniers : 1 company.

Total : 50 battalions.
49 squadrons.
72 guns.
8 Pioneer companies.
1 Pontonnier company.

52,736 men.
Left Wing.
Feldzengmeister [1] Graf. Gyulai.
Division. Field-Marshal-Lieut. Prince Aloys Liechtenstein. 3
Brigades= 12 battalions, 18 guns= 12,514 men.
Division. Field-Marshal-Lieut. Wiszenwolf. 3 Brigades= 13 battalions, 18 guns= 12,300 men.
Cavalry Division. Field-Marshal-Lieut. Freiherr-Lederer. 2 Brigades= 18 squadrons= 2,608 men.
8 Pioneer companies.
Total : 25 battalions.
18 squadrons.
36 guns.
8 Pioneer companies.

27,983 men.
Avance Abtheitung.
3rd Light Division. Field-Marshal Lieut. von Meszho. 2 Brigades=
5 battalions, 12 squadrons, 12 guns (strength not given).
Division. Field-Marshal-Lieut. Freiherr von Mayer. 3 Brigades
= 12 battalions, 18 guns (no strength given).
Division. Field-Marshal-Lieut. Prince Hohenlohe-Bartenstein.
2 Brigades= 8 battalions, 12 guns (no strength given).
Cavalry Brigade. Major-General Kuttalek von Ehrengreif. 2
Cuirassier regiments, 1 H. A. battery (6 guns).
1 Pioneer company.
Total : 20 battalions.
8 squadrons.
36 guns.
1 Pioneer company.
Artillery Reserve Park= 18 battalions= 108 guns.
Grand total Austrians = 127,000 men.

RUSSO-PRUSSIAN TROOPS.
Commander-in-Chief : General Graf. Barclay de Tolly.
Chief of Staff : Lt.-General Sabanjen.
Quarter-Master-General : Lt.-General von Diebitsch II.

Right Wing.
General Graf. Wittgenstein.
I Infantry Corps. Lt.-General Prince Gortschakow.
14th Infantry Division. Major-General von Helfreich.
2 Brigades, 8 battalions= 5,211 men.
5th Infantry Division. Major-General Messenzow.
2 Brigades, 13 battalions= 8,792 men.
Artillery : 3 batteries, 36 guns= 638 men.
II Infantry Corps. Lieut.-General Duke Eugène von Wurtemberg.
4th Infantry Division. Major-General Püschnitzki.
3 Brigades, 10 battalions= 5,370 men.
3rd Infantry Division. Major-General Prince Schachowski.
3 Brigades, 12 battalions= 6,598 men.
3 Batteries, 36 guns= 636 men.

---

1. *Feldzengmeister* means literally. Field Ordnance Officer, but has no connection with Ordnance matters; is merely a rank next below Field Marshal—the name dates from the Thirty Years' War.

157

Cavalry Corps.   Lieut.-General Graf. Peter Pahlen III.
Irregular Cavalry—Don Cossacks.
    4 regiments = 1,600 men.
    1st Hussar Division.   Major-General Milesinow.
    2 Brigades, 19 squadrons = 2,630 men.
Lancer Brigade.   Major-General Lisanewitch.
    3 regiments, 16 squadrons = 1,940 men.
Artillery : 2 batteries, 20 guns (6th Battery : 8 guns ; 7th Battery,
    12 guns).
Pioneers : 1 company.
Headquarter Guard.
    1 Dragoon regiment, 2nd Brigade Cossacks, 1 Landwehr battalion
    (Olonetz and Wologda) = 1,000 men.
Total : 45 battalions, 38 squadrons, 5 Cossack regiments, 92 guns,
    1 Pioneer company = 34,926 men.

Left Wing.

II Prussian Army Corps.   Lieut.-General von Kleist.
    Chief of Staff : Col. von Tippelskirch.
    Quarter-Master-General : Lieut.-Col. von Grolmann.
    10th Brigade.   Von. Pirch I.
        16 battalions, 4 squadrons, 8 guns = 8,026 men.
    9th Brigade.   Von. Klüx.
        10½ battalions, 4 squadrons, 8 guns = 8,021 men.
    12th Brigade.   Prince August von Preuszen.
        10 battalions, 2 squadrons, 8 guns = 7,172 men.
    11th Brigade.   Von. Ziethen.
        10¼ battalions, 6 squadrons, 8 guns = 8,743 men.
Reserve Cavalry.   Von Röder.
    Brigade.   Von Mutius.   Landwehr, 2 regiments.
    Brigade.   Laroche von Starkenfels.   Light, 3 regiments.
    Brigade.   Von Wrangel.   Cuirassiers, 3 regiments.
    Artillery.   2 H.A. batteries, 16 guns.

Reserve Artillery, 64 guns.
2 companies Pioneers.
Total : 41 battalions, 44 squadrons, 112 guns = 37,800 men (about).

Russo-Prussian Guards and Reserves.
Grand Duke Constantine.
Infantry.   General Graf. Miloradowitch.
III Infantry (Grenadier) Corps.   Lieut.-General Rajeovski.
2nd Grenadier Division.   Major-General Sulima.
    3 Brigades, 12 battalions = 6,756 men.
1st Grenadier Division.   Major-General Tschaglokow.
    3 Brigades, 12 battalions = 7,206 men.
Artillery.   2 batteries, 24 guns = 382 men.

V Infantry (Guard) Corps.   Lieut.-General Yermolow.
2nd Guard Division.   Major-General Udom I.
    2 brigades, 10 battalions = 5,941 men.
1st Guards Division.   Major-General Baron Rosen.
    2 brigades, 13 battalions = 7,725 men.
Artillery.   3 batteries, 36 guns = 632 men.

1st Cuirassiers Division.   Major-General Depreradowitch.
    2 Brigades, 19 squadrons = 2,428 men.
Light Cavalry Division.   Major-General Schewitch.
    22 squadrons = 2,345 men.
3rd Cuirassiers Division.   Major-General Duka.
    2 Brigades, 16 squadrons = 2,165 men.
Artillery.   2 batteries = 16 guns.
Irregular Cavalry.   3 regiments Don Cossacks.
Royal Prussian Guard Cavalry Brigade.   Col. von Werder.
    8 squadrons, 1 battery (8 guns) = 1,606 men.

Grand Total:

	Bat-talions.	Squad.rons.	Guns.	Cossack Regts.		Men.
Austrian	107	117	290	—	=	127,345
Russians	92	109	274	15	=	82,062
Prussian	47½	52	128	—	=	44,907
	246½	278	692	15		254,404

Royal Prussian Guard Infantry Brigade. Lieut.-Colonel von Alvensleben.
6 battalions, 2 rifle companies, 8 guns= 5,485 men.
Cavalry Corps. Lieut.-General Prince Galitzin.
4th Cuirassier Division. Kritow.
2 brigades, 14 squadrons= 1,860 men.

The preceding orders of battle deserve attentive study, *as they mark very distinctly the transition period between the old and the modern systems of organization.* In the grouping of the Prussian forces we see the germ of the methods which in 1866 and 1870 acquired such renown that they became the universal model for all civilized nations. But in the Austrian and Russian commands we find confusion worse confounded; no definite idea seems to attach to any particular name, and one can easily imagine the confusion possible in attempting to direct the operations of a force of 200,000 men in which the terms "Corps," "Division," *"Abtheilung"*[1] appear to be applied without any reference to the magnitude or the importance of the units thus designated. Where units, not being numbered, are known by the names of their Leaders only, which of course are liable to change after every action, the confusion is endless.

I am far from defending the excessive regularity which is characteristic of the modern German method, which leads the superficial thinker to believe that 300,000 armed men cannot fight at all unless grouped in Army Corps, of three Divisions, each of two Brigades, etc., or whatever the pre-

---

1. *Abtheilung* means literally "detachment," but the word "detachment" was also frequently used in its French form to signify any body of troops broken off from their usual connection. It is generally translated by the word "group," but group also is used for bodies of all magnitudes. In modern military German *"abtheilung"* is used to designate a group of three or four batteries and was translated into English by the absurd word "Brigade-Division," a term which has fortunately become obsolete.

vailing fashion of the day may be. There seems no adequate reason for facilitating the work of the enemy's Intelligence Department in the field by this simplification of forms, and every reason why one should not furnish each subordinate Commander with a weapon of the same weight and material, no matter what his capacity may be. But between the hopeless chaos of the Bohemian Army, and the Chinese like precision of modern European forces, there seems room for a happy mean, which is to be found in a reversion to the Napoleonic method, in which the strength of the principal units varies with the skill of its Commander. A Bertrand or Reynier would have been hopelessly overpowered by the responsibility of a five Division command, whilst a Davoût would have been wasted on only two.

Clausewitz's saying should always be remembered, "there is no worse sub-division of a force possible than one of three parts—except only one of two." The ideal command will be found in one of four or five, according to the ability of the Commander, and in support of this contention the conduct of the Prussian Corps Commanders on the battlefields of 1866 and 1870 may be cited. Almost invariably, as soon as the bullets began to fly they passed over the Divisional Commanders entirely, and sent orders direct to the Brigades, thus unconsciously reverting to the type established in the old Silesian Army of 1813.

CHAPTER 7
Katzbach—Dresden—Kulm

By the terms of the Armistice a neutral zone some twenty miles in width had been established between the contending forces in Silesia. As the period for the resumption of hostilities (August 17) drew near, it became important to Blücher to be in close touch with the enemy to his front so as to have timely warning of his possible manoeuvres. To obtain this the neutral zone must be traversed, consequently a pretext for infringing the letter of the Armistice had, to be found.

It was fortunate for the Prussians that this was not far to seek. The French at the front had been suffering much from want of food and forage, and had from time to time entered the neutral zone in small parties in search of supplies. On August 13, a number of these foraging parties being reported, Blücher, affecting to regard them as a prelude to the more formal fighting to be expected after the 17th, ordered the whole Silesian Army forward, in a line of four Corps, one marching on each available road. The advance Cavalry soon came in contact with the French, who were completely off their guard. When on the following day they learnt that strong Infantry columns were moving against them on a front of thirty miles (being in entire ignorance of the great detachment Blücher had made to the Bohemian Army) they naturally concluded that the troops in front of them were the advance of the whole Silesian army in force, and concentrated backwards, not without some confusion. Thanks to this, the Prussians gained several minor advantages in the fighting which ensued, facts which served materially to raise the *moral* of the new German levies.

But from the first the want of experience in the Prussian Staff began to create friction. Thus on the very first day, Blücher and Gneisenau separated from each other the better to superintend their observations over the enemy's front, with the result that they did not meet again until late in the afternoon, hence the issue of orders was delayed to such a degree that, the troops did not begin to move until the following noon, and then had to march late into the night to reach their destinations.

Each day, fresh causes of delay arose, and the resistance of the French became more obstinate. Thus every march ended as a night march, and the weather being abominable, the whole Army suffered so severely that when on the morning of August 20, Blücher found himself in presence of the whole massed forces of his adversary across the Bober river, it only needed the sound of the cheers which announced Napoleon's arrival to assume command of the French Army, to decide him to retreat forthwith.

Then followed a series of most obstinately contested rearguard actions in which every day many fives were lost, and by the 25th the whole Silesian Army was in a condition bordering on dissolution. The *Landwehr* men had deserted in masses to their homes, Langeron, St. Priest, and even Sacken, were complaining bitterly of the way their troops were being wasted, and Yorck found the position so intolerable that he actually wrote to the King, begging the latter to relieve him of his command, as he could not look on and see his troops ruined by the incompetence of the Staff.

Blücher's own position was almost impossible; he hated retiring even more than did his subordinates, with whom and with the men he thoroughly sympathized. But he was compelled to submit, by the terms of his appointment, to the dictation of Gneisenau. For a moment, it is said that he contemplated the extreme step of displacing Gneisenau and appointing von Kaetzler in his place, but learning that Napoleon was no longer in personal control of the French pursuit, on the night of the 24th he decided to turn upon his enemy. Accordingly he issued orders for an advance towards the Katzbach, which resulted on the 26th in the general action which has since borne that name.[1]

Now it was that good luck favoured him in a most unusual degree. The Katzbach springing from high ground in the mountains to the southward, rose during the battle in a sudden flood. Carrying away many of the bridges, and destroying all the fords, it cut the French Army in half as it was moving to the attack of the Prussian position. At the critical moment Blücher ordered an advance of his right wing, and the muskets being too wet for effective use, the battle was practically decided by cold steel, the French, overwhelmed by the fanatical impetuosity of the Prussian assault, being driven into the river, where many hundreds were carried away and drowned. This brilliant victory was the making of Blücher and the Prussian Army. Indeed it was the salvation of the whole Allied cause, for news of it was brought to the Royal Headquarters at a moment when the general situation seemed hopeless, and more than a possibility existed that Austria might enter into a separate treaty with Napoleon and abandon the coalition altogether.

We must now return to Napoleon, and the measures he was taking to utilize to their full the advantages of the "interior lines" on which he stood as regards his adversaries.

---

1. This battle affords another instance of slipshod staff service, The Emperor had ordered Macdonald to advance on the 25th, but simultaneously he had directed Ney to report to him. The order, however, was so worded that Ney conceived that it applied both to him in person and his Corps, which he promptly set in motion to join the Emperor. But the III Corps numbered five Divisions, say 50,000 men, and without them Macdonald could not execute his orders, and twenty-four hours were lost before the mistake could be made good.

The disposition of his troops in itself must be pronounced a model for all time; for notwithstanding its great extent he could concentrate on its centre or on either wing a greater force than his enemies could possibly bring against him, and provided Dresden could be relied on to hold out for six or seven days, he felt completely master of the situation. *It had however the disadvantage inherent in all defensive arrangements, viz. that the initiative lay in the hands of his adversary.* Napoleon's first view had been that the Allies might attempt a direct attack on the line of the Riesengebirge, and to that end, he had occupied, and caused to be fortified, all the passes leading over them into the plains. Being for the time quite independent of his communications with France, and relying solely on Dresden, he desired nothing better than an advance of the Bohemian Army against Leipzig, and he seems hardly to have hoped for so much good fortune as actually befell him.

His first act on learning of Blücher's advance was to reconnoitre personally the line of the passes he had taken up, in order to assure himself that he would have ample time to deal with the Silesian Army before the Austrians could arrive. Being satisfied on that point by a reconnaissance made on the 18th, by which he learnt that troops had actually marched from Blücher's command to Bohemia, he issued orders to Macdonald (now in chief command of the "Army of the Bober", as the troops facing Blücher were called) to have the troops ready for his personal command on the morning of the 20th. He then spent the 19th in reviewing troops and dealing with the endless details of administration, with which, in the absence of a properly trained Staff, he was compelled to burden himself.

His arrival on the morning of the 20th caused, as we have seen, Blücher's immediate retreat; and as information came in which made clear the weakness of the Silesian Army, and hence the exceeding improbability that he could compel it to stand for a decisive battle, he handed over command again to Macdonald on the 22nd, and returned to Görlitz, taking his Guards with him, there to await further developments.

Meanwhile the Allied Headquarters in Bohemia had fallen completely into the trap he had laid for them. Believing Napoleon to be vitally concerned in the retention of his communications with France, they had, after many conferences, decided on a concentric advance over the mountains across Saxony to Leipzig, their right watching Dresden, about the defences, or perhaps the spirit which animated its defenders, they appear to have been better informed than was the Emperor. The detachments of the Prussian and Russian forces made by the Silesian Army having arrived within supporting distance, the march was started by every available road from the Elbe to Leipzig, only two of which, however, were made and metalled roads. The others were little more than mountain tracks, scarped roughly out of the side of the hills with gradients up to 1 in 4 (15°) and no attempt to improve them appears to have been made throughout the campaign.

The natural consequence was that the heads of the several Corps could not keep their alignment, and those unfortunate enough to be on the bad roads (and these were the majority) were worn out in their efforts to keep up with their luckier comrades. During the 20th the news of Napoleon's personal appearance at the pass of Zittau (on the 18th) created something approaching consternation, for many supposed it preluded an advance on Prague, which to the strategists of that day must have loomed up as the prelude to an appalling calamity. Everyone in any way entitled to give advice (Moreau and Jomini amongst them) at once assembled, and a discussion ensued in which the only man who appears to have maintained an attitude of decorous modesty was Prince Schwarzenberg, the Commander-in-Chief. Ultimately (though it is impossible to trace with whom the idea originated), the meeting decided that the whole Army should bring up its left shoulders, and swing in upon Dresden, which was to be attacked and stormed before Napoleon could return. Orders to this effect were prepared and issued. This wheel to the left, however, threw the bulk of the columns from the main roads and tracks upon cross-tracks, which, running transverse to the drainage lines of the district, presented a succession of up and down gradients of the worst description, thus throwing an increased strain upon the already over-taxed marching powers of the Allied troops, and though during the course of August 25 the heads of the columns, driving the French outposts before them, closed in on the city, the tails were left straggling far behind.

In the afternoon of that day Schwarzenberg, with the three Monarchs and their retinues, rode up to the heights above Räcknitz overlooking the town, and here again a long discussion took place. Eventually it was decided that the forenoon of the following day should be devoted to concentrating the several columns for battle, and that the attack itself should begin about 4 p.m.; the actual signal for movement was to be given by three gun shots.

The crowd now separated to prepare the necessary orders. How long Schwarzenberg's Staff required to draft out the prolix and exhaustive memorandum that was to guide every detail of execution, it is impossible to specify. I should imagine that it would take a man well acquainted with the ground at least three hours, and after that it had to be dictated, and sent out to about 200,000 men. When, if ever, its pith reached the company officers must remain undecided; but it must have been late in the following day, if at all.

Next morning, the Monarchs were out early to watch the preparations, when about 9 a.m., through the veil of mist which still lay over the valley, a great cheer of *Vive l'Empereur* surged out of the town, and in a moment the words "too late" were on everyone's lips.

Only the King of Prussia stood out, emphasizing the point that for an Army of 200,000 men to back down before the mere threat of a shout, was unprecedented; it could hardly be called War at all. Again a long discussion, prolonged into the afternoon. Finally counsels of prudence prevailed. It was decided to retreat, and Schwarzenberg rode off to prepare the necessary orders for this step. The precise time of this decision cannot be fixed, but the fact remains that at 4 p.m. no orders had reached the troops, who had all arrived at their appointed places, and were waiting for the word to advance. Suddenly, someone, who it never can now be ascertained, fired the signal guns, and the attack on Dresden began.

We must now return to Napoleon, whom at we left on the 23rd at Görlitz.

Contact with the Bohemian advance had been established by the French troops watching the passes, early on the 22nd, and their reports reached Headquarters during the 23rd. For the moment the Emperor's thoughts turned towards Prague, as the Allies had anticipated that they would, but presently the letters from St. Cyr became alarming and his attention was directed into another channel. The situation appeared to him as follows. Distance precluded any immediate danger from the Silesian Army, but to make assurance doubly sure, he ordered Macdonald to advance, and attack anything that attempted to stand against him. It was this order in fact which brought on the battle of the Katzbach. Presuming his most explicit instructions to have been obeyed, Dresden was amply secured against any attempt to carry it by storm. At the worst its defenders could retire into the fortified bridgehead of the Neustadt and so prolong their defence by days. To St. Cyr, together with his own Corps, he had given authority to call upon the II Corps (Victor) and I Corps (Vandamme) for assistance, both of which could reach him in twenty-four hours.

But St. Cyr did not mention whether he had as yet made any use of this authority, or indeed whether he intended to use it at all.

For the moment he appears to have made no definite plan. Calling up the Guards to Görlitz, where his own Headquarters lay, he wrote an encouraging letter to St. Cyr, pointing out the strength of his position, and the time during which it could be held, also intimating that he would march himself to his assistance, and could if necessary arrive on the 25th. But at the same time a doubt seems to have crossed his mind as to whether the fortifications which he had ordered were in fact as far advanced as they ought to have been. He therefore wrote another letter to Rogniat, his Chief Engineer, couched in a very different tone, sending also Gourgaud, one of his most trusted personal Staff, to report on the whole situation to him direct. Then he penned the following very remarkable letter to Vandamme:

> I have just received a letter from Marshal St. Cyr dated August 22, 11 p.m., telling me that a Russian Corps is advancing through Peterswalde, and that the whole, Austrian Army is upon him. If this is the case, then march your whole Corps by the shortest way to Dresden. I assume that the 23rd and 2nd Divisions are already on their way there. If, however, this movement is not yet begun, then march them at once to Stolpen. Send the Division of the young Guard, the Cavalry Division of Lefebvre-Desnouettes there also, leaving only a rearguard to cover your movement, which will be relieved by the troops of Prince Poniatowski.

It seems quite clear from the above that when he began to write he was still dominated by the plan of bringing direct support to St. Cyr, but in the middle of his letter a fresh idea strikes him, and without pausing for a moment to consider that its execution involves depriving St. Cyr of the troops already assigned to him, he changes the destination of Vandamme's command as a preliminary to the execution of a manœuvre which he does not deign to develop here to his subordinates, but which in its consequences must have surpassed in renown the greatest feat he ever actually accomplished. A few hours later (early morning of 24th) he writes to Maret in Paris, authorizing him to warn the press to prepare the public for great victories in the corning days.

> My plan is to go to Stolpen. My Army will be united there tomorrow (25th). I will spend the 26th in preparations and allow my columns to close up. In the night of the 26th I cross the river at Königstein with 100,000 men, and occupy the camp of Pirna. I shall have two bridges ready to throw at Pirna.
>
> Either the enemy has taken his line of operations by Peterswalde to Dresden (in that case I shall be with my united Army in his rear, and it will take him four to five days to concentrate). Or, he has gone by the road from Komotau to Leipzig, then he will retire on Komotau, and I shall be nearer to Prague than he is, and shall march there.

Immediately afterwards the following orders were issued.

> Prince Poniatowski remains in his position at the defiles at Gabel and Georgenthal. The Duke of Belluno (Victor, II Corps) will reach the district between Stolpen and Bautzen on the 25th, and arrange to cross the Elbe on the morning of the 26th, at a point to be shown to him hereafter.
>
> The Duke of Ragusa (Marmont, VI Corps) will reach Reichenbach today, Bischofswerda tomorrow, and cross the Elbe on the 26th.

There are no orders for the Guard, but they would march under his own eyes. During the day he rode to Bautzen, and proceeded at night to Stolpen, where he arrived about daybreak.

Here disagreeable news awaited him. First came that of Oudinot's defeat by the North Army at Groszbeeren near

Berlin; but the report is vague and inconclusive, and he appears to have attached little importance to it. Next came the unwelcome intelligence that a regiment of Westphalian Cavalry had deserted to the enemy. This was the first overt act betraying the spirit of his German contingents. The loss of the actual men was of small account, but the news they happened to carry to the Allies proved subsequently of importance. To prevent such occurrences in the future he ordered all the Westphalian Cavalry to be dismounted. He then transferred their horses to French commands. Followed other disturbing communications from Dresden. At 11 p.m. Gourgaud returned with the news that if the enemy had pressed their attack home that afternoon, the town would already have fallen, but they had delayed it and there was yet a chance that if the Emperor returned at once the city might be saved.

Then at last Napoleon's resolution failed. Cancelling all previous orders, he directed all available troops (except Vandamme's) by the nearest roads to Dresden, and riding on himself in advance, he galloped over the bridge, where his unexpected arrival gave rise to the cheers which so terrified the Allies. Close behind him came the leading files of the Guard. These had marched from Stolpen at 4 a.m. and moving in dense rendezvous formations (mass of columns on a company front at half distance generally, only the guns being upon the road), they went straight across country, and by noon 26 battalions were already in Dresden. At nightfall this number had risen to 68 battalions, 117 squadrons, 534 guns. In what order the mounted arms actually arrived is uncertain, most of them probably between noon and 5 p.m., the distance (17½ miles) being of course for them inconsiderable. But the march as a whole remains one of the most remarkable on record, and one can only imagine how such a feat must have upset the calculations of his opponents, who judging the situation by the ordinary rules of the game, could never have believed it possible to transfer a whole Army of this magnitude by a single road in little more than twelve hours.

The Corps of Victor and Marmont (II and VI) reached Stolpen during the night, and pushing on at daybreak next morning arrived in time to take part in the renewed fighting of the 27th. Considering the material of which these troops were composed—young and inexperienced conscripts—and considering also the fact that the Guards were always better fed and cared for than were any other of the units, their performance is even more remarkable, for they had traversed a distance of 120 miles in four days; by a single road and through a country practically destitute of supplies. They had had no proper night quarters, they had simply lain down and slept wherever the column halted. Yet as a body they marched in full of swing and life, and remained in touch with the enemy for the next forty-eight hours.

How many of them fell out and were left along the road it is impossible nowadays to ascertain. *The essence of the whole matter is that enough of these raw immature boys actually reached the field in sufficiently good order to be controlled and directed in action.*

The details of the battle which now ensued possess but little interest at the present day. About 4 p.m. of the 26th the columns of the Allies attacked with considerable vigour, driving in the principal advance posts of the French, but before they could recover from the confusion inseparable from such success, the French Reserves issued forth from the wide openings intentionally arranged to facilitate such counterstrokes, and attacking in their turn with the bayonet, promptly recaptured their lost positions. Generally, when darkness put a stop to the fighting, the troops on both sides occupied much the same augment as they had held at starting. But during the night Napoleon made his arrangements for a great counterstroke against the left of the Allies.

Murat was given the command of the Cavalry Corps of Latour Maubourg, and of Pajol's Cavalry Division, 68 squadrons in all, with 30 guns, and of Victor's Corps and Teste's Division, 44 battalions, totalling some 25,000 men with 76 guns. These were ordered to work round the enemy's outer, *i.e.* left, flank, whilst the fight was continued along the front, and fortune favoured this plan in a singular manner. Shortly after midnight the rain came down in sheets, turning all the country off the roads in the low grounds into a morass; on the plateaus between the water courses, the drainage being better, the going was at any rate fair. Whilst Victor and Teste attacked the Austrians in front, Murat took his Cavalry by road right round the prolongation of the enemy's front, and emerging suddenly out of the cover on which their left rested, literally swept away the whole wing, for owing to the continuous rain the flintlocks of the Infantry proved useless, and squares without fire power were entirely inadequate against the momentum of his charges.

The effect of this success, however, was only local, for owing to the configuration of the ground, the centre of the Allied Army still remained intact, as it was separated from the beaten wing by a broad and deep ravine.

But the Allies' Commander-in-Chief had already determined that want of both food and ammunition rendered retreat imperative, and during the afternoon the fighting was only continued to gain time for the necessary dispositions. In fact, the battle came to an end by the mutual exhaustion of both sides. Men and horses were alike so worn out that anything approaching an effective charge across the rain-sodden fields was out of the question. Napoleon knew that Vandamme had already reached Pirna, thus closing the shortest and best line of retreat available for the Allies, and he felt confident that after a night's rest his troops would soon overtake any start the enemy might have obtained.

About 5 p.m. the Emperor rode back into Dresden, drenched to the skin, and worn out, but still in good spirits and hopeful for the morrow, as his letter written the same evening to Cambacères sufficiently proves:

> I am so tired and so busy that I cannot write at length .
> . . . the Duke of Bassano will do so for me. Affairs here
> are very satisfactory.

At dinner in the palace of the King of Saxony, he was most cheerful, and after commiserating his unfortunate father-in-law, the Emperor of Austria, he said: "Today the rain saved the enemy from complete destruction. I had intended to storm the whole line of heights. However, we shall be in Bohemia before my colleagues (the three monarchs) after all." Then a little later he added: "I am well satisfied with the results of the day; but when I am not present, things go wrong. All the troops sent towards Berlin have been beaten, and I fear for Macdonald. He is brave and good, but unfortunate." A true prediction, as it happened.

Early next morning the French were in motion; the Emperor riding out towards their left flank to reconnoitre in person. Everywhere the advancing troops came upon signs of a hasty retreat, and of terrible suffering in the ranks of the Allies. Whole Austrian battalions had moved off leaving their muskets still piled in ranks, and men too exhausted to drag themselves further lay in the fields, while some were found suffocated face downwards in the deep mud. It seemed impossible that the Army could have gone far. Indeed, the Cavalry reports indicated that the retreat had been made along all the roads over the mountains, far to the south. Therefore, it was a reasonable conclusion that Vandamme with his 40,000 men at Pirna (in command of the only first-class road in the district) could reach the exits from the mountain passes about Teplitz in time to intercept the bulk of the enemy's forces. St. Cyr and the Young Guard marching by the same good road would be within supporting distance if anything untoward happened, and Marmont following on directly was to hang upon the enemy's rear, whilst Murat with Victor and the Cavalry tried to work round their southern flank.

As at the same time satisfactory news arrived from Vandamme, who had attacked and driven back the flanking detachment under the Duke Eugène of Wurtemberg (left to hold the passages of the Elbe at Pirna on the previous day), the Emperor concluded he could give the Young Guard a much needed rest. He accordingly ordered them to bivouac where they stood, and getting into his coach drove back to Dresden, where at 8.30 p.m. the news of Macdonald's defeat on the Katzbach was handed to him.

The escape of the right wing of the Allies from the trap thus laid for them is one of the most curious episodes in military history and deserves to be treated with more detail than is usually accorded to it.

Duke Eugène of Wurtemberg, in reply to his repeated requests for reinforcements, found himself suddenly superseded in his command by the arrival of General Ostermann with a whole Division of the Russian Guards. Ostermann, however, was practically out of his mind, and in charge of two attendants. But in his lucid intervals he agreed not to interfere with the Duke's command. Unfortunately he insisted on riding with him, and when any question concerning his Guards arose, his senses appear to have deserted him entirely.

The Duke saw quite clearly that Vandamme was endeavouring to reach the defile of Peterswalde, where the road on which he and Kleist's Corps of Prussians were marching opens into the great Pirna-Teplitz *chaussée*. He therefore implored Ostermann to give him the assistance of the Guards to attack, and hold Vandamme in check throughout the day, pointing out the vital importance to the whole Army of keeping him at bay.

But Ostermann was not at all touched by these arguments, nor were his subordinates either. The Guards were the Tsar's own personal property, and their officers felt that they would never be forgiven if the bright paint on their Ruler's expensive toy should be tarnished or chipped in the rough game of war. Deaf to all remonstrances from Duke Eugène, Ostermann marched off leaving the Duke to do the best he could with his very inadequate means to carry out his plan of obstructing Vandamme's movements.

In the meantime a number of coincidences arose. The King of Prussia had ridden on alone from the night quarters of the Monarchs, and had chosen a path along a spur of the mountains from whence he had a full view over the plains below. The sound of heavy firing arising from the action between the Duke's little column and Vandamme's advance guard, reached his ears, and he saw in a moment the inevitable consequences if the French General should succeed in driving his opponents beyond the defile of Priesten, through which at that moment Ostermann's column was retiring.

The King at once galloped after the madman, and by a happy inspiration pointed out to the Russian Staff the danger in which their Sovereign, still within the mountains, would be placed if Priesten was not defended by the Guard; this appeal proved efficient. Ostermann or his representative counter-marched the column, and took up a retaining position, ready to receive the Duke of Wurtemberg as he fell back.

Simultaneously, almost, the Tsar himself had left Headquarters by another path running along a spur parallel to that on which the King of Prussia was riding. The sound of firing caught his attention also, and in his turn he took in the situation at a glance. From his spur of the mountains he could not see Ostermann, however. What he did see was another large body of Allied troops away in the plains, and he rode after them to bring them back to the Priesten position.

They turned out to be Colloredo's Austrian Corps of 14 Battalions and 18 guns moving in direct compliance with Schwarzenberg's orders, issued the night before, and

Colloredo did not see his way to acceding at once to the Imperial request that he should reinforce Ostermann at Priesten. Fortunately at this moment Metternich, the Austrian Prime Minister, arrived, in a very dejected frame of mind. Learning from the Emperor Alexander's own lips the yet greater danger that threatened if the French under Vandamme were not promptly opposed, he took the responsibility of ordering Colloredo back to Priesten, at which place the latter arrived so opportunely that Vandamme found himself compelled to delay his final attack until the following morning, as in the long and confused day's fighting his command had straggled a good deal.

When the battle was renewed the next morning the two opponents were fairly well matched, about 46,000 victory inspired French against some 50,000 Austrians and Russians. Vandamme had taken up his position in the little village of Kulm in face of the Priesten defile. About 1 p.m. he had sent forward practically all his troops for a decisive effort. They seemed to be carrying everything before them, when suddenly there was an outburst of heavy firing and cheers to his rear. The next moment a mass of Prussians burst into the village, taking the French force completely in reverse, Vandamme was captured with his Staff, and his command was completely destroyed or dispersed.

We must now retrace our steps to follow the vicissitudes of this Prussian Corps which had appeared so exactly at the right moment.

The Corps of Kleist, some 10,000 strong, had been left in touch with the main French Army in the vicinity of Dohna, and in its retreat had found itself gradually shouldered off successive lines of escape by Vandamme's advance.

On the night of August 29, Kleist found himself in desperate straits. The one roadway still open to him was so completely blocked by broken-down transport that twenty-four hours would hardly have sufficed to clear it for the passage of troops, so he decided to cut himself adrift from the map and trust to luck to find a way across country. Calling his officers together, he told them that he intended to fight his way through the French, sword in hand, and his plucky resolution was greeted with cheers. At daybreak next morning his columns climbed the spur which lay between them and the Pirna-Teplitz road. They then moved northwards along it, till they struck a country track leading down a ravine which ultimately debouched upon the above-named road. Scrambling down through the forests, for some 2,000 feet, they at length reached it. Finding it entirely unoccupied they promptly proceeded to reform their columns, and then marched along it towards the sound of the firing which came from the village of Kulm.

Rounding a turn in the road, they saw the battle raging in front of them. Being as yet entirely unobserved, they formed up for attack and rushed the village, almost before the French were aware of their presence.

There can be little doubt that this fortunate intervention changed the whole fate of the campaign, and the credit for it belongs in fairly equal proportions to the Duke of Wurtemberg for his courage, to the King of Prussia and the Tsar for their timely interference, and to Kleist for his daring acceptance of responsibility which meant much more in those days of rigid adherence to prescription, than it would do at present.

The proximate cause which led to this complete disappointment of all Napoleon's hopes, lay undoubtedly in St. Cyr's failure to avail himself of the authority delegated to him by Napoleon to call Vandamme to his assistance. How a man of St. Cyr's distinction, who had himself exercised independent command on several occasions, and whose writings prove him to have been one of the first strategists of his day, could have blundered in this extraordinary manner is one of those insoluble problems in human psychology which from time to time arise and upset all calculations and all designs. If Vandamme, in obedience to St. Cyr's summons, had been already on the march to Dresden when Napoleon sat down to write the letter quoted above, no question as to the safety of that town could possibly have arisen; while the Emperor would have been free to carry out his design of placing 100,000 men in rear of the Allies on August 27, as he wrote to Maret, then in Paris.

But the question then arises whether but for his uncertainty as to Vandamme's movements, the plan would have occurred to him at all? Evidently it was not in his mind when he began his letter. It flashed across him as he wrote, and so blinded him for the moment that he failed to notice that by ordering Vandamme back to Stolpen he created the very situation which ultimately caused its abandonment. The letter strikes me as conclusive evidence of an absolutely tired mind. It is so carelessly worded that it is almost incredible that he can have read it over a second time, and the following letter confirms the impression; for Napoleon, when under the full control of his genius, would never have contemplated a dual objective, and still less would he have talked about the occupation of Prague as long as his enemy's undefeated Field Army was in existence.

The next questions are—How did this fatigue originate? Was its cause preventable? and is not the fact of its appearance in itself the best proof of the failure of the Commander to have realized in this instance the whole scope of all that his career had previously taught the world of War. It has been said by many critics that in this campaign the Emperor no longer gave proof of that all compelling energy in execution, of that ceaseless attention to detail, and that absolute disregard of his personal comfort which had distinguished him in his earlier days? But Major Friedrichs, with all the documentary evidence now in existence before him, has no difficulty in rebutting these accusations. It is absolutely clear that Napoleon was ceaselessly on the move; the marvel is how he ever found time to either sleep or write. But all this only confirms the point I propose to bring forward, *viz.*, *that he had never intellectually realized the secrets of his own success.*

Hitherto, when in command of Armies approximating in magnitude to those he was now directing, *he had always acted on the offensive,* with a clear and definite purpose before him, a purpose which no possible threat or movement of his enemies could possibly disturb. Where they moved in darkness, distracted by every passing rumour and threat, he marched confidently forward, convinced of his power of beating down all opposition on the battlefield itself, when and wherever he might encounter them. *Now, however, events had thrown him upon the defensive, and at once the increased difficulty of the situation forced itself upon his attention.*

It was not only that his Cavalry failed him, for that had happened to him before, notably in 1806 and 1809. No, *the essential difficulty now lay in the fact that the initiative had passed from his hands to those of his adversary, and therefore he was compelled to wait until the latter gave him an opening, of which to take advantage.* That opening he certainly saw when he penned his letter to Vandamme, *but it is clear from the measures he suggested that his inspiration did not suffice to show him the best way in which to avail himself of the chance given to him;* and this simply because his mind was at the time too weary to work out intellectually the full possibilities of the situation.

Presumably since he had actually prepared three bridges at or near Pirna, and held two others in hand to throw across the river as occasion might require—the new road, or roads (I can only find mention of one) which he had ordered to be constructed, must have been good enough for 100,000 men to pass along them, during the twenty-four hours he allowed himself. But there was only one road available in continuation to Hellendorf (the objective he mentions in his letters to Maret) and in the defiles of that district, his Army could hardly move on a broad front, as it had done from Bautzen and Stolpen on Dresden. His 100,000 men, therefore, would have taken about as long to concentrate to the front as the Austrians would have taken to counter-march to their rear. Moreover, the latter would have held the best graded road in the district in their possession, *viz.*, from Freiburg via Dux to Teplitz, by which to manœuvre against the French flank.

I therefore submit *that had Napoleons conduct of war been the result of intellectual study, and not the intuition of genius,* a far simpler, and more effective plan would have followed from the intellectual application of the forms which he had himself invented, which depended for their efficacy on the superior marching powers of the French troops under certain conditions, all of which presented themselves in the case now before us.

In the campaigns of 1807 and 1812 in Poland and Russia, the formation "in battalion square of 200,000 men," had broken down because, owing essentially to difficulties of supply, he had not been able to outmarch his enemy and compel him to stand and give battle. If he had struck towards Prague whilst the Austrians and Allies were still in the vicinity, it is possible that he might have caught them up. The harvest was just being gathered on the southern slopes of the Bohemian mountains, and as the whole district had escaped the ravages of war for the last fifty years, supplies therefore would have been abundant. On the other hand, however, there was no particular reason why the Allies should stand to be beaten, when they had the whole of Austria and Hungary in which to manœuvre and escape.

When once, however, the columns of the Bohemian Army had entangled themselves in the defiles leading to Saxony, they were at Napoleon's mercy had he, as before said, only realized intellectually the secret of his own successes, *viz.*, *superior mobility.* Leaving only a weak rear guard under Ney to cover his withdrawal the IV and XI Corps, preceded by

Poniatowski (VIII Corps) as an advance guard, should have been set in motion via Zittau, Graben, Leitmeritz, Lobositz, on Teplitz, which they would have reached during the course of August 28, having started on the 24th, the distance being less than what the II and VI Corps actually accomplished in their march to Dresden, and the gradients better than those they had surmounted.

The II and VI Corps, with the Guards, would have reached Hellendorf in the same time; while Dresden, with St. Cyr and Vandamme would have been perfectly safe for forty-eight hours, even assuming that the town was ever in danger. Further, whilst the centre and right attacked and held the enemy, the left would have taken the Teplitz-Dux-Freiburg road, and would have swung in on the enemy's rear, wherever and however he might have placed himself.

Here we should have seen the "lozenge" or "square" formation at its best; wheeling about a fixed point (Dresden) attacking an enemy who practically had no retreat open to him, and therefore could not evade the blow, but would have to counter-march under almost impossible conditions. Meanwhile the French themselves would have lived on their enemies' magazines and trains, with the additional power of supplying themselves with any stores that the Allies' forethought had not already provided, via the line of the Elbe in the first instance, the road through Dippoldiswalde next, and then in succession the Freiburg and the great Leipzig road. Then, having completed the wheel, they would have reached the Elbe again on the fourth day from Teplitz, in ample time to meet either Bernadotte's or Blücher's Army had the necessity for this arisen, though after the crushing defeat of the Allies this movement must have entailed, such a contingency would appear most improbable.

By this movement, all uncertainty would have been at once allayed, for once the troops were in motion, the enemy's possible eccentricities could no longer matter. If by any chance they had penetrated Napoleon's design in time to mass themselves against the French left, they must by so doing have weakened their own left, when the French left about Teplitz became the pivot, and the wheel would have been executed in the inverse direction. If they had massed against the centre, then the wings would have swung in like the jaws of a cracker, and a greater blow with more decisive consequences must have been the result.

Chapter 8

Gross Beeren—Dennewitz

We left Napoleon on the afternoon of August 28 driving back from Pirna, well satisfied with the promise of the day, and pleased with the number of trophies and prisoners which were hourly arriving from the front. A second report from Oudinot relating to his defeat at Gross Beeren, received about noon, was insufficient to disturb his serenity, which remained proof even against the far more serious news of Macdonald's defeat on the Katzbach, and of Girard's reverse at Hagelesberg, which reached him during the evening of the same day. For once, however, no immediate step was taken to remedy either misfortune, and we are amazed to find the great Emperor, hitherto the very incarnation of rapid decision, faltering for thirty-six hours before deciding on his next move in the great game. During these hours he dictated his strategical situation.[1] These are so absolutely opposed in their contents and arrangement to anything one could previously have conceived as coming from the mind of this great Master of men and War, that many doubts have been cast on their authenticity. But as the German General Staff have accepted them, we may bow to their authority.

They are too long for reproduction, but briefly they discuss at considerable length two alternatives, *viz.*, a march with

---

1. *Notes sur la situation générale de mes affaires.*

the main Army on Prague, or a march, with Oudinot's command largely reinforced, on Berlin, and the marvel is that the Emperor's decision could have wavered for a moment. For Prague, it was already too late, from the moment when he had said, "I see nothing more to do" at Pirna; and, as already pointed out, the direction of Prague held out no hope of a decision. The Bohemian Army could always run away faster than he could follow them. Berlin, on the other hand, held out all the fascination of his original northern plan, heightened by the satisfaction to be derived from administering prompt chastisement to Bernadotte, to say nothing of the more real advantage of a fresh country in which to operate, and finally the relief of the fortresses of Danzig, Küstrin and Frankfurt.

In the early hours of August 30 Napoleon's resolution was taken to march on Berlin, and Berthier was instructed to order the Guards and the Cavalry back from the Bohemian frontier, across the Elbe at Dresden, and towards Groszenhain. In consequence of these orders, during the afternoon the troops began filing ceaselessly over the bridges.

But already the foundations on which this plan had been based, flimsy enough at the best, had crumbled to pieces under the stubborn logic of events.

Late in the evening the Emperor received a despairing appeal from Macdonald, imploring his presence to re-establish order and discipline in his defeated command, and at 2 a.m. on the 31st came the news of Vandamme's catastrophe at Kulm. A few hours later, General Corbineau, who, with a few cavalry men, had cut his way through the enemy, appeared, and was at once admitted to the Emperor's presence. What followed is thus described by Baron Fain in his *Manuscript de 1813* (II, p. 319) which I translate from Major Freidrichs' work (Vol. II, p. 8):

Napoleon received the detailed account of the disaster without betraying any sign of his feelings. What he could not understand was how Vandamme could have allowed himself to be tempted so far in pursuit. For an Army in retreat one must either build a golden bridge or oppose its progress with a dam of steel and iron. Walking up and down the room in deepest thought, he asked Berthier: 'Can we have written anything which could have thus misled him? Fetch me your order book. Fain, show me my notes. Let us see what we said.'

The Major-General brought his order book, the Cabinet Secretary the notes, and together they went through the papers. They found nothing which could have justified the unfortunate General in leaving his position at Peterswalde.

This was perhaps the most magnificent exhibition of his histrionic talent that Napoleon ever gave, and of such exhibitions not a few have been recorded. But the facts were too hard to be explained away, and the Headquarters Staff failed to be impressed with it. General von Gersdorf, (Saxon) writing in his diary the same evening summed up the situation as follows:

The impression made by the successes at Dresden and by Moreau's death have been wiped out; all consequences these events might have entailed are simply-destroyed. Confidence grows in the camp of the Allies in proportion as it sinks with us. The Emperor is very quiet; I hardly like to write 'depressed,' but very pensive, curiously he is not irritable; the spirit of Headquarters generally bears the stamp of the time."[1]

As an immediate consequence of these disasters the movement on Berlin was suspended. Nothing whatever was done on August 31. On September 1 the Emperor replied to Macdonald's appeal (received on the night of the 30th) ordering

1. *Freidrichs,* Vol. II. p. 9.

him to hold on to Görlitz at all costs, meanwhile holding out the hope of his own arrival with reinforcements. He also sent Ney to Wittenberg to relieve Oudinot of his command and to restore order in the disorganized debris which after the defeat of Gross Beeren had rallied about, that place. But his chief attention appears to have been devoted to preparing the troops about Dresden to meet a renewed offensive on the part of the Allies.

With this object St. Cyr (XIV) was ordered to remain at Pirna. Victor (II) was sent to Freiberg, and Marmont (VI), Mortier (Guards) and Latour-Maubourg's Cavalry were united around Dresden as a central reserve. Lobau received the command of the wreck of Vandamme's Corps, (I) which by using Teste's Division as a nucleus was raised to about 14,000 men and 66 guns (obtained by drafts from other commands) and 300 sabres.

It was now too late to carry out his march on Berlin in the manner he had originally designed. On the other hand, it was quite impossible for him to remain where he was, and since the outpost reports gave no hope that the "Grand Army"—as it had come to be called—would obligingly step down into the plains to be beaten, he now resolved to move the Guards, the VI Corps and his Headquarters to a central position equally convenient to reinforce Macdonald, Ney or Murat, whom he determined to leave in chief command at Dresden.

This central position Napoleon found in the little village of Hoyerswerda, where the road from Dresden to Berlin via Cottbus intersects a second-class road coming from Wittenberg via Leutenberg to Bautzen. During September 2nd Berthier wrote to Ney the following sketch of the situation, also an outline of Ney's special mission, to supplement such verbal instructions as the latter had taken with him from his personal interview with the Emperor, which seem to have been of the vaguest description:

We have just received news from the Duke of Reggio (Oudinot) who has seen fit to fall back to within two marches of Wittenberg. The consequences of this untimely movement are that General Tauentzien and a strong body of Cossacks have turned towards Lückau and Bautzen, where they threaten Macdonald's communications. It is really difficult to show less head than Oudinot.

Everything is being set in motion for Hoyerswerda, where the Emperor and Headquarters will arrive on the 4th. You must march on the 4th, and be in Baruth on September 6. On that day the Emperor will place a Corps at Lückau which can join you. From Baruth it is only three marches to Berlin. Communication with the Emperor will thus be established, and the attack on Berlin can take place on the 9th or 10th. The whole division of Cossacks, and all this mass of inferior *Landwehr* Infantry will everywhere be thrown back on Berlin if your march is made in a determined manner. *You will understand the necessity for rapid action in order to draw advantage from the confusion of the Bohemian Army,* which is sure to set itself in motion as soon as it learns of the Emperor's move. Oudinot never attacked the enemy, and was clever enough to engage only one of his Corps. If he had gone at him resolutely he would have overrun him everywhere.

The above deserves attentive study, as it was the immediate cause of the catastrophe of Dennewitz, which in its consequences proved the most serious reverse which the French had as yet sustained. Ney, who, in fact (in his usual impulsive manner), had started for Wittenberg with no definite instructions, had found Oudinot's troops in extreme disorder, penned in with their back against the Elbe by the whole of the Army of the North, which Bernadotte had very skilfully disposed so as to hide its weak effectives.

The Emperor in his instructions never alludes to the position of this enemy at all, and they were clearly written under the impression that no serious opposition could be opposed to the prescribed march on Baruth by the Army of the North. But Ney saw only his orders, and with the fate of Oudinot before his eyes, determined not to fall into the error of weak execution, which the context of Berthier's memoranda so strongly condemns.

Having re-established some measure of order among the troops (during September 3 and 4), on the morning of the 5th Ney broke out of his position with his whole three Corps. He moved straight across country in masses towards Zahna to gain the Lückau-Bautzen road. The weather being clear and dry, the dense dust clouds stirred up by this formidable array gave Bernadotte ample warning of its coming, and though Tauentzien's weak Corps of *Landwehr*, on whom the blow of Ney's advance directly fell, were easily thrown back in dire confusion, all the remainder of his Army, Bülow, Wintzengerode and the Swedes, were immediately set in motion to move parallel to the French and head them off if possible from Jüterbogk. A cloud of Cossacks, and a low roll of the ground concealed this movement from Ney, whose troops bivouacked for the night around Zahna, quite unaware that a formidable enemy was gathering within five miles of their left flank.

Early the next morning the march was renewed, the IV Corps (Bertrand) leading, followed by the VII (Reynier) and XII (Oudinot), each marching in mass of Divisions, the Artillery only on the road.

Tauentzien had bivouacked near Dennewitz and had spent the night in restoring order amongst his *Landwehr*, and with such success that, confident of prompt support, he was able to take up a position effectively barring the further progress of the French, though he had barely 10,000 men under arms. *This is worth noting, for it shows how readily raw troops can be* rallied, *even from serious panic, if they only know what they are fighting for.* Still, an encounter against such odds could only end one way, and after about two hours' fighting the *Landwehr* were faltering in every direction, when Bülow's men appeared on the flank of the French IV Corps. Their attack at once stopped the progress of the latter, and now it was Bertrand who was thrown on the defensive. The arrival of the VII Corps again turned the scale, but fresh Prussian battalions turning up, the left flank of the French gave way, and their position was only saved by the appearance of the leading troops of the XII Corps.

But just as the whole mass of this new command were preparing for a final counterstroke against the Allies in order to finish the day, Ney, who all this time had been watching the battle with Bertrand's men, and knowing nothing of what was happening on his extreme left, sent orders to Oudinot to continue his march to the front. The latter, who since his supersession by Ney in the command of the Army, had been in that worst of tempers in which a man confines himself to the literal obedience of his orders—however much circumstances may have altered and his own common sense may apprehend this fact—called off all his troops, and in spite of Reynier's most urgent remonstrances he resumed his march to join Ney, passing close along the rear of the hardly pressed VII Corps.

Punishment was not long delayed, for ever since morning the Russians and Swedes had been pressing their march to the utmost, and warned of the urgency of the case, their Horse Artillery and Cavalry had hurried on far in advance. Almost as the last of the XÜ Corps quitted the line, the storm burst upon the exhausted VII Corps. An advance of every available gun to case shot range preluded the approach of a perfect hurricane of horsemen, before whom the French broke, and pursuers and pursued poured down the slopes upon the flanks of Oudinot's masses.

The defeat was absolutely catastrophic! A wild panic seized the French, and for the next few days Ney's command ceased to exist.

We must now return to the Emperor, whom we left completing his arrangements for the defence of Dresden. His orders on this subject to Rogniat (his Chief Engineer) dated September 3 remain as masterpieces for all time, and equally so are his instructions to St. Cyr of the same date. Thus, having provided for every contingency as far as human foresight could well go, he started on the afternoon of the 3rd to overtake the Guards and Reserves already on their way to Hoyerswerda (about forty miles north-east of Dresden). But at the last moment a report from Macdonald, dispatched the previous evening, was handed in to him, which again shattered the basis of his whole design.

Briefly, Macdonald again represented his command as absolutely out of hand; he could find no one to support him in his efforts to maintain discipline, and only the Emperor's presence could avert utter disaster.

This time there was no hesitation. Orders went to all the marching columns to change direction towards Bautzen. Ney was warned of the Emperor's alteration of his destination, which might postpone his march on Berlin until Blücher's Army had been disposed of; but Ney was to continue the execution of his own march on Baruth to be able to back up the Emperor the moment he returned, and Macdonald was warned to have all his troops in readiness for inspection early next morning, so that the Emperor could ride down the front in half an hour. Then the moment the Guards and Latour Maubourg arrived, which would be between 2 and 3 p.m., the Emperor proposed to attack the enemy wherever he found him.

Napoleon slept that night at Gross Harthau, and rode on in the early morning of September 4 towards Bautzen. That he had expected to find things in a bad way is clear from the steps he had already taken to meet the most urgent necessities, and to replenish both arms and equipment. But what he really encountered was worse than anyone had dreamt of imagining. Swarms of bare-footed, unarmed and starving stragglers met him as he rode; and there was no food to give them, for a big convoy of provisions and ammunition had been intercepted by a raiding command from Blücher's Army, and only its smoking remains lay by the roadside. And here, at length, the Emperor lost his usual self-control. A miserable dog ran out and yapped at his horse as he rode by; he drew his pistol on the poor wretch, but the pistol missed fire, and in a rage he flung it at the animal. Then he rode on in gloomy silence, until he met Macdonald and his staff outside Bautzen. Then his temper completely overmastered him. Turning on Sebastiani (Commander of the 2nd Cavalry Corps), he upbraided him in such unmeasured terms that Caulaincourt and the Staff had to close round him to shut off the undignified scene. Thence he rode on to Hochkirch, where the heads of columns of the Silesian Army were seen approaching. At these he hurled the nearest of his troops at hand, who now, suddenly ashamed of themselves and anxious to retrieve their reputation under their Emperor's eyes, attacked with such vigour that Blücher and his Generals immediately detected the presence of the Master, and at once ordered a retreat behind the Lobau river. This was carried out successfully, thanks to the desperate fighting of their respective rear guards.

He then spent the night at Hochkirch, and rode off early in the morning to the Wohlauer hill to reconnoitre the enemy's position in person. But the morning reports made it clear that Blücher was in full retreat, and despairing of bringing him to action, suspecting also a plot to draw him further from Dresden, he returned to Bautzen with the Guards, and learning from Ney that he would leave Wittenberg for Jütebogh on the 5th, orders were issued for the Guards and VI Corps to march on the 6th to Hoyerswerda.

Bt two hours after this decision had been taken again he felt compelled to alter their destination, for further alarmist reports from St. Cyr at Dresden reached him. Seemingly forgetting all the orders which he had issued to meet the contingency of a fresh advance on the part of the Bohemian Army, he hesitated, changed his mind, and forthwith couriers were sent after the Guards and the 1st Cavalry Corps to change their direction from Hoyerswerda to Dresden. Only Marmont (VI Corps) was to continue his march on Kamenz.

Of the many strange situations in this Campaign, this is perhaps the most difficult to unravel. St. Cyr's reports contain nothing to show that anything had occurred in excess of what Napoleon's precautions had been intended to provide for. Hence, if his calculations before leaving Dresden had been correct, there was no particular reason for this extraordinary alarm. Further, even if St. Cyr's story had been many times darker, and the Bohemian Army had, in fact, been in full march over the mountains, this would have been only a repetition of the situation he had already faced and provided for on the 23rd of the previous month. Then he had written, in reply to similar dismal forebodings on the part of St. Cyr:

> If the Bohemian Army crosses the mountains and advances into Saxony, in that case I will wish them *bon voyage;* they will come back quicker than they went.

His troops at this moment occupied almost identically the same position as on the night of August 25, and if Dresden really was in jeopardy, surely the shortest way to its relief would have been by one side of the triangle from Bautzen to Teplitz, rather than by the two sides from Bautzen to Dresden, Dresden-Teplitz.

Before leaving Bautzen the following order was published to the Army:

Every soldier who leaves his colours betrays the first of his duties.

His Majesty therefore orders—

Soldiers who leave the colours without sufficient reason will be decimated. The Corps Commanders, therefore, every time they have collected ten stragglers will cause them to draw lots, and one of them is to be shot.

On the evening of the 6th Napoleon reached Dresden, where he found renewed reports from St. Cyr to the effect that "The Austrians were advancing by Altenberg, the Prussians and Russians by Borna[1] and Berggieszhübel, where they had already arrived." There was no indication at all of the forces they had deployed, still less as to whether they were moving on Chemnitz and Freiberg, both points of very great importance. The Emperor expressed his dissatisfaction at the incompetence of the whole Intelligence Service. To clear up the situation he sent Victor's Corps in support of St. Cyr to Dohna, on the 7th, and rode out next morning at the head of the Guards to conduct a reconnaissance in person.

It is now time to return to the Bohemian Army, which we left at the moment when the tide of its misfortune had been suddenly arrested by its victory over Vandamme at Kulm (August 30), and when the news of Gross Beeren and the Katzbach, both of which had been received during the previous twenty-four hours, had stiffened its drooping spirits.

But though all idea of further retreat was abandoned, a halt to re-establish order in the several commands, and to issue fresh ammunition and equipments, especially boots (for nearly half the Army was by this time barefooted) was urgently necessary.

The abortive expedition had entailed a loss in killed, wounded, prisoners and sick of some 45,000 men, of which 9,000 men with 600 horses fell upon the Prussians, nearly 30

---

1. Not to be confused with the "Borna" south of Leipzig.

per cent, of their original effective. But in spite of this heavy punishment, endured day by day under the depressing conditions of continuous retreat, the Commanding Officers were all able to report that in their conduct the men had shown both goodwill and devotion beyond all expectation or praise.

The breakdown of the commissariat had been complete, and the Russians, particularly the Cossacks, had sought to make good the deficiencies in their supply by living on the inhabitants, and robbing them right and left. So serious, indeed, were the disturbances and sufferings created by these half-civilized horsemen that flying columns had to be organized, which the inhabitants of the country gladly joined, to hunt down these marauders and hang them out of hand. It may be mentioned here that these same troops proved equally troublesome in the rear of all three Armies, and that behind the Silesian Army they formed themselves into organised bands of brigands, who waylaid, stripped and murdered every civilian and even officer who fell into their hands.

The chief result of these victories, *viz.*, Kulm, Gross Beeren and Katzbach, on the future of the campaign was, however, to confirm for good and all the allegiance of Austria to the Triple Alliance. Up to the very day of the battle of Kulm, Metternich had been carrying on diplomatic relations with Napoleon, and both the Prussians and Russians felt that he might desert the common cause at a moment's notice. Now decisively he flung diplomacy to the winds, and in a final communication to the French Emperor formulated such preposterous demands for the conclusion of peace that nothing but hopeless defeat could have enabled the latter even to consider them.

Under the depressing influences of defeat a letter had been despatched to Blücher on August 29, calling upon him to march with 50,000 men (*i.e.*, more than half his command as it stood) to the assistance of the Bohemian Army, and notwithstanding the victory of Kulm, the demand was not withdrawn. Thence a long correspondence arose, which reveals very completely the entire want of anything approaching organized co-operation in determining the ultimate issue of the campaign.

The letter to Blücher did not convey an absolute order, merely a royal wish, leaving, as far as these things can be left, the final decision to depend on the circumstances prevailing at the Silesian Headquarters on delivery of the document.

Now at that moment, unknown, of course, to Blücher, Napoleon had actually gathered together his forces for his often proposed march on Berlin, and Ney had received his orders to fall upon Bernadotte and overwhelm him, and it was only Blücher's resolute pursuit, or, better, pressure upon Macdonald's command which caused the Emperor to abandon his design and turn upon Blücher.

Meanwhile, Bernadotte, able to gauge the Emperor's mind far better than did any other of his colleagues, was painfully aware of the imminent danger which threatened his command in its isolated position right in the path of the Emperor's march on Berlin, which he had divined, from the first, as Napoleon's immediate reply to the defeat of Oudinot at Gross Beeren. Judging by the light of the fuller knowledge now available, there can be no doubt that this counterstroke, had it been carried out, must have been decisive of the whole campaign. Having marched right over the North Army, relieved Danzig and the Oder fortresses, and then with Davoût having reopened communications with Magdeburg, the Emperor again would have been in touch with all the resources of France, and the 32nd Military Division. Indeed, he might have renewed the campaign with an assured numerical superiority and with a wholly re-established military prestige. But not an inkling of this possibility seems to have dawned on the Allied Headquarters, who called on Blücher for reinforcements, which would only have added to the existing congestion of the district in which they stood. These were refused by Blücher, not on the grounds of Bernadotte's danger and consequent claim on the loyalty of his nearest comrade, but because neither he nor Gneisenau desired to have their freedom hampered by the loss of half their troops.

Blücher's private autograph letter to Knesebeck is so characteristic that I reproduce it with its original spelling; it was sent under cover with the formal dispatch:

Um des allgemeinen wohl und Besten, bewahren, si mich vor einer Vereinigung mit der groszen armeh; was soll eine solche ungeheure masse auf einen gleichsam ausgezerten terrain, hir will ich wirksahn sein und kann ich nützlich werden, weiche ich von einen den Kronprinzen von Schweden mitgetheilten operations Plan ab, so kriegt er sicher, staht dasz er nu mit starken chritt vorwerts geht; solte Napoleon nach Boehmen Inneingehn wollen, so musz man ihn in Boehmen vernichten, ich glaube aber, dasz er die Elbe verlast wenn man gut manouvrirt.[1]

Blücher

Hernhut, den 13 Sept., 1813

It will be noticed that in this letter Blücher does speak of a combined operation with the Crown Prince of Sweden. But Major Buhle von Lilienstein, who carried this dispatch, had verbal instructions to point out to the Allied Sovereigns, not the imminence of the danger which threatened the Crown Prince and his troops as long as Napoleon held the passages over the Elbe, but that no reliance could be placed on the loyalty of the Crown Prince himself unless Blücher and Gneisenau were at hand to drive him; and, in anticipation, it

---

1. "For the general good and welfare preserve me from a junction with the great Army; what can such an enormous mass do in such a famine-stricken desert? Here I can be active and useful; if I deviate from the plan agreed upon with the Crown Prince of Sweden he is sure to get licked, instead of going forward at once with confidence; if Napoleon enters Bohemia, he must be destroyed in Bohemia, but I believe that he will leave the Elbe if we manoeuvre well."

may be added, that a secret intrigue was already on foot by which on the approach of the Silesian Army Bülow and Tauentzien were to refuse obedience to the Prince and transfer their forces to Blücher's command, in case the latter hesitated to press operations with the energy they desired.

Bernadotte's conduct in every campaign has always remained an insoluble problem to all students. His absence from the battlefield of Jena at the critical moment, and his amazing indiscreetness at Wagram (for which the Emperor had actually ordered him to be tried by court martial) had cast suspicion on him in many quarters. Now the fact that neither at Gross Beeren nor Dennewitz had he nor his Swedes taken part in either battle had completely shaken the confidence of the Prussians in his courage and his loyalty. Yet in the present instance those suspicions prove to have been unfounded, and Major Friedrichs (who is the first to discuss the situation with adequate documentary evidence at his disposal) is able to establish Bernadotte's *bona fides* at this period of the campaign beyond all reasonable doubt. In so far as he appeared to be lacking in enterprise, the explanation is that he knew his wily adversary and the nature of his own danger far better than could any of his critics.

Fortunately for the Allies, events moved far more rapidly than the correspondence, but it was necessary to emphasize the point at this period of the narrative in order to throw light upon the undercurrents of intrigue which hampered the movements of the three Armies.

Returning now to the Bohemian Headquarters, we find the troops sufficiently re-established. to resume operations on September 5. Accordingly, the columns again penetrated into the mountains by the same roads which they had used previously, and it was the fighting which ensued as the advance guards came in contact with the French outposts that led St. Cyr to send off his alarmist reports to the Emperor at Bautzen.

But on the 6th, and whilst the first line of their Army was still in close touch with St. Cyr's troops, news reached the Allies from an unimpeachable source that Napoleon had again turned against Blücher, taking with him the bulk of his troops. Now it was that while still uncertain as to the reply Blücher would give to the demand for 50,000 men, the Headquarters decided to march 60,000, by Aussig, Leitmeritz and Rumburg, to his support, and the movement was actually initiated.

We must pause a moment to contemplate the amazing spectacle which would have been presented had Blücher already complied with the Allied Sovereigns' request; 60,000 men marching north on one road, whilst parallel to them and only a few miles distant 50,000 marched south on another highway; 110,000 men neutralized, and Napoleon in the middle of them to take advantage of this incredible opportunity.

But hardly had the troops started their march than the situation once more underwent an entire change, for Napoleon was again reported as in full march for Dresden, and, as we have seen, the report was confirmed by his appearance in person during the course of September 8 at the head of his Guards in that city.

A retreat and concentration was immediately decided upon, and the whole Bohemian Army was ordered to be drawn up for battle on a plateau covering Teplitz and the exits from the mountains.

The retreat of the advance detachments involved severe fighting, but by the evening of September 9 the whole of the Russian and Prussian contingents had taken up their positions, and on the morning of the 10th Napoleon, from the heights of the Geiersberg, was able to look down upon, and almost count, the individual men opposed to him.

Reconnaissances were at once pushed out to find roads suitable for the passage of artillery across the ravine lying at his feet, but when in the evening Drouot, his most trusted Artillery Commander, returned with the report that the plateau was utterly inaccessible to that arm, he made up his mind to abandon the attempt to force on a battle. Leaving St. Cyr to make every show of concentration, to send out working parties to ostentatiously repair the roads, etc., he returned to Dresden to attend more closely to the situation which had arisen out of Ney's defeat at Dennewitz, the full magnitude of which had at length struck home to him.

St. Cyr in his *Memoirs* has criticized this decision most adversely, drawing unfavourable comparisons between the man who crossed the St. Bernard without field artillery in 1800 when entering Italy, and the Emperor who now hesitated because his guns could not follow the Infantry. But this criticism only serves to show how little his contemporaries had fathomed the secret of their Leader, or grasped the profound change in the spirit of their own troops and the character of their opponents. In 1800 the French Infantry still fought with Republican fanaticism, the Long Service Armies of Austria by routine. Now the situation was entirely reversed, and the French could only hope to beat their enemies when artillery fire had done its work. To bring up adequate masses of guns for this purpose on to the plateau being impossible, no decisive action could be hoped for, and only a decisive victory could be of use to the Emperor in his present situation.

Arrived in Dresden, Napoleon immediately issued orders transferring the Administrative Bureaus of the Army from Dresden to Torgau, which seems to indicate that for the moment a policy of concentration against the Northern Army, whilst still unsupported, flashed through his mind. But if this was the case, the idea was only temporary, for next morning (September 12) he ordered Marmont from Kamenz to Grossenhain, and sent Murat with the 1st and 5th Cavalry Corps to join him.

Immediately this movement served to cover the transit of a convoy of 15,000 cwt. of flour up the river into Dresden, but it might also have served as a preliminary for a renewed offensive against the Army of the North, and was appreciated in that spirit by Bernadotte.

The latter, after his victory over Ney at Dennewitz, had detailed Tauentzien to observe the French who had fallen back on Torgau, and Bülow was told off to besiege Wittenberg, whilst the Swedes moved down stream on Rosslau. Wintzingerode and Woronzow were at Zerbst, and Bernadotte was being strongly urged by his Prussian subordinates to pass at any rate one Corps of his Army over the Elbe to operate on the French communications, a step he had refused to take until Wittenberg was in his possession. His resolution had all but led to open mutiny on the part of the Prussians, as already noticed above, but Napoleon's threat from Dresden towards Grossenhain so completely vindicated his judgment, that it was impossible to cross the river as long as the Emperor was free to debouch from Dresden, Meissen or Torgau, that this opposition was for the time at least withdrawn, and more harmonious relations were established in his command.

But a fresh offensive by the Bohemian Advance of Army on September 14 against St. Cyr caused the Emperor to change his plans again, and on the 15th he marched with two Divisions of the young Guard to Pirna in the hope of surprising the Allies in an unfavourable position. This desire, however, was disappointed. The Allies immediately began their retreat, contesting every position desperately, and concentrating ultimately near Kulm, where they appeared as ready to accept battle once more.

On the 17th Napoleon rode out to reconnoitre from the mountains near Nollendorf, but fog and rain hindered all observations until midday. The attack was then begun, but a Prussian Corps defended the advance posts so resolutely that hardly any ground had been gained when a tremendous downpour of rain put a stop to the fighting about 5 p.m.

On the 18th the Emperor again rode out to reconnoitre in person. The air being clear he could see every detail of the enemy's position, and he noted particularly the stream of their reinforcements arriving. Reluctantly he ordered the Guards back to Pirna, and leaving Lobau and St. Cyr to reoccupy their former positions he returned to Pirna, where for the next few days (during which ceaseless rain made operations impossible) he remained secluded in his chambers, striving to grapple intellectually with the tide of misfortunes that now began to pour in upon him.

From the south came the news that the Austrians had surprised and captured (during the night of September 17-18) the garrison of Freiberg; from the west he heard that Merseburg, with a garrison of 1,800 men, had surrendered to a partisan commando under Thielmann and Mensdorf, and finally from Ney came the report, premature though it happened to be, that Bernadotte with 80,000 men had crossed the Elbe at Rosslau.

To add to all this, the condition of the French troops was deplorable; their rations had been cut down from 28 oz. of bread to 8 oz. (raised again, it is true, by the successful introduction of the 15,000 cwt. of flour into Dresden to 24 oz.); but this supply was already beginning to give out, and the district offered absolutely nothing but potatoes. Meat had scarcely been seen for weeks, and the half starved men, exposed to the inclement weather night after night in rain-sodden bivouacs, were melting away by battalions.

Since the resumption of hostilities, he had lost not less than 150,000 men, 300 guns and a huge amount of war material. Upwards of 50,000 sick and wounded still crowded the hospitals, whence it was said only one man in ten came out alive; but yet, notwithstanding this accumulation of catastrophes, the iron will of this extraordinary man would not bow to the inevitable and sacrifice Dresden, although this city not only was of no further military advantage to him, but on the contrary was a source of gravest danger. And for this reason. His foes had now approached so close on both sides that he had no longer room to manoeuvre, and all the time Bernadotte lay in his direct path to ultimate victory, simply waiting to be destroyed. Here the Ruler undoubtedly sacrificed strategy to the apparent interests of his dynasty.

On September 21 Napoleon returned again to Dresden, and on the 22nd, taking with him his Guards, as usual, he joined Macdonald, who still faced Blücher, and drove the latter back on the 23rd to the strong position he had already prepared about Bautzen, where this time it was apparent the old fellow had determined to make a stand. But at this moment Ney sent word that the Northern Army had thrown a bridge over the Elbe at Wartenburg, close above Wittenberg, and that he feared to be cut off both from Torgau and Dresden. On receipt of this news (again a premature report) the Emperor at length gave orders for a general withdrawal of the whole of Macdonald's command to the left bank of the Elbe, giving out that it was his intention to afford them the few days' rest which they so urgently needed. In accordance with this intention, by September 27 the French Army occupied the following positions:

I. At Dresden   (a)   on the right bank of the Elbe—

XI Corps (Macdonald) at Weissig
2nd Cavalry Corps (Sebastiani) at Pillnitz
III Corps (Souham), Dresden and on the road to Grossenhain

(b)   On the left bank of the Elbe—

V Corps (Lauriston) around Dresden
The Guards, Dresden and Pirna

II. Facing the Bohemian Army

> I Corps (Lobau) at Berggiesshübel
>
> XIV Corps (St. Cyr). 43rd Division, Pirna and Pillnitz, 42nd Division, Königstein. 44th and 45th Division, Borna and Dippoldiswalde
>
> II Corps (Victor) at Freiberg
>
> VIII Corps (Poniatowski) and 4th Cavalry Corps (Kellermann) at Waldheim

III. Facing the North Army—

> IV Corps (Bertrand), Kemberg and Schleesen
>
> VII Corps (Reynier) and 3rd Cavalry Corps(Arighi) (exclusive Lorge's Division) in Dessau, Wörlitz and Oranienbaum

IV. Covering the Elbe north of Dresden—

> VI Corps (Marmont) between Meissen and Würzen
>
> 1st Cavalry Corps (Latour) between Grossenhain, Meissen and Schildau.
>
> 5th Cavalry Corps (L'Héritier) at Meissen

V. To guard the rearward connections—

> 2nd Guard Cavalry Division and Leipzig Corps of Observation (Margaron) under the command of Lèfebvre-Desnouëttes, at Altenberg Dombrowski's Division and Cavalry Division (Lorge) on the march across the Mulde

VI. On march to reinforce the Army—

> IX Corps (Augereau) from Würzburg towards the Saar
>
> March Division (Lefol) from Erfurt to the Saale

For the next few days the Emperor was fully occupied in reorganizing the Army and issuing instructions for placing the towns along his main line of retreat in a state of defence.

Bridgeheads were ordered to be constructed at all important river passages, and all sick and wounded were sent back towards France.

On September 27 a decree was published calling up 120,000 men of the contingents of 1812-11-10 who had hitherto not been drawn as conscripts, and 160,000 men of the contingent of 1815 were ordered to be enrolled in advance.

In order to obtain more unity in the command of the troops destined to confront the Bohemian Army, the King of Naples (Murat) was ordered to take over the II, V and VIII Corps with the 5th Cavalry Corps, and one Division of the 1st Cavalry Corps, and to establish his Headquarters at Freiberg.

If this disposition is carefully studied it will be seen that it is in itself a masterpiece of defensive strategy, for each wing is strong enough to resist, for a couple of days, any force which could reasonably be brought against it, and in that time the strong central reserve could support it with overwhelming numbers.

Unfortunately, however, it suffered from one grave defect, which nullified all its many advantages, *viz.*, *the whole army was starving, and the men no longer possessed the physical strength with which to meet their Emperor's demands.* Yet there is no sign that the idea of retreat had received serious consideration, for such precautionary orders as had been issued are quite insufficient to justify this interpretation.

In the meantime, the Silesian Army, released from the pressure hitherto exercised upon it by Macdonald's command, had been quick to take advantage of its freedom for action. Posting Sacken to watch Dresden in the vicinity of Grossenhain, Blücher had directed the whole of the remainder of his forces by Kamenz-Liebenswerda towards Wittenberg, hoping by his presence to drag the Crown Prince of Sweden into activity.

As already pointed out above, the relations between the two commands had been none of the best, and neither

Gneisenau nor Blücher had recognized the extreme danger of Bernadotte's position, hence they seem to have been quite unprepared for the cordial reception their proposals evoked from him. In the Silesian Army itself the idea of undertaking this dangerous flank march across Napoleon's front, and abandoning all their communications, evoked the liveliest anxiety. The Russian Commissary-General, Count Thuyl, protested solemnly, and demanded that the proposed plan should be submitted to a council of all the Generals in the command, but Blücher here showed the firmness of his character, and dismissed the suggestion with an absolute refusal to hold any council of war. The risk was extreme, and he knew it; but since the Bohemian Army could not make up its collective mind, and Bernadotte alone was powerless to move, he determined to assert his initiative, and to drag the whole three Armies into motion by the force of accomplished facts. He was precisely one of those strong men who do not hesitate to recognize bedrock facts, and chief amongst these is the truth *that communications were made for Armies, not Armies for communications,* and an Army with its own country behind it can never be severed from a base, though that base need not necessarily be the most convenient one. Well it was for the cause of the Allies that at length such a man had been found to compel them to act; for the novelty of the march was so far beyond anything that Napoleon had ever anticipated from any one of his enemies, that he was completely deceived as to its object when the news reached him, which it did very promptly.

He at once interpreted it as a preliminary to an attack on Dresden from the north-west, between Meissen and Grossenhain, in order to avoid all the difficulties of manoeuvring presented by the forest land towards Bautzen, and whilst making dispositions to deal with this threat, he allowed Blücher to continue his march undisturbed, with the result that on October 2 the Silesian Army had concentrated in the immediate vicinity of Wartenburg, and had begun preparations to force the passage of the Elbe at that point.

The attention of the French had already been directed to this spot by an attempt at a crossing made by detachments of the North Army on September 20, and Bertrand had provided abundantly, as he thought, for its defence. But though an engineer, he had forgotten to consult the levels of the river, and had not realized that a fall of a couple of feet might render his position untenable.

The Prussians, though in their own country, seem to have been equally, or indeed more, ignorant of the nature of the ground. They had selected the point of passage from the best map available (a very bad one), and on paper it appeared to "present all the most desirable conditions for a river crossing", *viz.*, a great re-entrant bend towards their side (the north), bushes and trees to mask operations, and a convenient tributary (the Elster)[1] in which to collect their material. But the surface within the re-entrant was completely hidden from view by dense undergrowth, and the existence of an old branch of the river, only fordable with difficulty at a couple of points, seems to have been quite unknown to them. It was on the existence of this old riverbed that Bertrand relied; he had personally reconnoitred the ground in the spring, and believed it to be quite impassable. But he had not noticed that the river itself was at the moment considerably lower than usual.

The Prussians, after several hours of desperate fighting across it at close quarters, ultimately did find unsuspected passages, and pouring through them with both Cavalry and Artillery, by almost unequalled efforts (the result of a fighting spirit which would not be denied) they turned the French right, defeated all counter attacks by case fire and Cavalry charges, and before nightfall were complete masters of the enemy's position.

---

1. Not to be confounded with the "Elster" at Leipzig.

Tactical details are beyond the scope of this present work, but the extraordinary tenacity of purpose these troops displayed requires to be brought out to show how infinitely more important is the *spirit with which men fight than the forms in which they have been trained, or the strategic relations of their fronts to one another.*

The troops, line and *Landwehr*, side by side, had been marching and fighting incessantly for six weeks, alternately in advance and in retreat, and their privations had been most serious. Yorck's Corps, to whom the credit of the whole day belongs, had shrunk, notwithstanding frequent reinforcements, from 38,484 to 12,000 in the morning of the battle, and of these 12,000, 1,600 were left on the field. But this loss does not fairly indicate the strain actually endured by those personally engaged at the decisive points of the fighting line, for in the densely wooded ground only the heads of the columns could be hotly engaged; but these seem to have been shot away again and again, and it was their absolute refusal to admit defeat that in the end turned the scale in their favour.

STRENGTH OF FRENCH ARMY—END OF SEPTEMBER, 1813

	Men.	Guns.
(a) In and around Dresden—		
Imperial Guard	44,000	202
XI Corps. Macdonald	25,000	68
I Corps. Lobau	12,500	47
XIV Corps. St. Cyr	28,000	60
2nd Cavalry Corps. Sebastiani	6,800	12
	116,300	389
(b) Along the Elbe, Strehla to Meissen—		
III Crops. Souham	15,000	61
(c) On the Mulde, Eilenburg to Bitterfeld—		
IV Corps. Bertrand	15,500	32
VII Corps. Reynier	22,000	48
Dombrowski's Cavalry Division	3,500	8
Detachment. 3rd Cavalry Corps.	2,500	6
VI Corps. Marmont	22,500	82
1st Cavalry Corps. Latour Maubourg (less Berckheim's Division)	6,000	27
	71,700	203

(d) Between Altenberg and Freiberg—

II Corps. Victor	16,000	55
V Corps. Lauriston	14,200	53
VIII Corps. Poniatowski	6,900	30
4th Cavalry Corps	3,000	12
Berckheim's Division from 1st Cavalry Corps	1,000	6
	43,550	156

(e) In and around Leipzig—

	Men.	Guns.
Corps of Observation under General Margaron	5,700	16
Cavalry Division. Lorge	1,500	6
	7,200	22

(f) Between Weissenfels and Naumburg—

A mixed Cavalry Corps under Lefèbvre-Desnouëttes	5,000	6

(g) On the march to Leipzig—

IX Corps. Augereau	9,200	64
Cavalry Division. Milhaud	3,500	—
	12,700	14

Grand total . . 256,000 men, 784 guns.

CHAPTER 11

Leipzig

Whilst the Silesian Army completed the passage of the Elbe at Wartenburg, Bernadotte with the North Army crossed some twenty miles lower down at Rosslau. The two Armies were thus within easy supporting distance of each other, and together constituted a fairly formidable fighting force of about 150,000 men. The Bohemian Army could still put 180,000 in the field, and Napoleon at Dresden lay midway between them with— including reinforcements— about 260,000. From a purely military standpoint, therefore, his situation had not been altered for the worse, since he no longer had three separate forces to contend against; and by continuing to play the game of "interior lines" he could still mass a numerical superiority against either of the Allied enemies, sufficient at least to ensure a victory under normal conditions; but absolutely overwhelming when multiplied in fighting power by the magnetism of his personal presence and command.

The catastrophe of Leipzig, however, was so complete and dramatic, and its final causes were so obvious, that posterity has invariably treated the subject as if the end must have been as clearly evident to the actors then as it is to us now; and instead of seeing in the Emperor a great General playing his part, still with absolute confidence in his final triumph, it has insisted on regarding him as a hunted animal trying to evade the toils of its trappers, and it has magnified every little incident which has seemed to intensify the animal's sufferings.

Viewed from this standpoint, it is indeed easy to pick holes in Napoleon's strategy; for his blindness and his hesitation to seize the many chances of escape which the blunders of the Allies provided for him, become quite unaccountable. But when we picture the Emperor to ourselves as still supremely conscious of his own superiority over his opponents, one can only marvel at the fertility of resource, and the unswerving confidence in his Army and in its marching and fighting powers which he maintained under the most depressing surroundings.

From his point of view his position at Dresden had become intolerable only because he could not get at his enemies to smash them utterly.

The Bohemian Mountains formed no suitable setting for a great tactical decision, but once he could tempt the Bohemian Army out into the plains he knew them to be far too slow to evade the consequences of his determined onslaught. On receiving the news of the passage of the Elbe, on the night of October 4, he at once issued orders for the troops about Dresden to march next day towards Meissen, placing the XI, VI and III Corps, together with the 3rd Cavalry Corps, provisionally under Ney's command. He then prepared to follow himself at the head of the Guards, the XI Corps, and 2nd Cavalry Corps next morning (October 7).

His general idea is best expressed in the following letter to Marmont:

> I shall be this evening with 80,000 men in Meissen; my advance guard at the cross roads from Leipzig and Torgau, and I shall decide upon which to choose according to the reports I receive . . . . I intend to move to Torgau and from thence down the right bank of the Elbe in order to cut

the enemy off and seize all his bridges without the necessity of attacking his bridgeheads. An advance down the left bank would have the inconvenience that the enemy might retreat across the river and thus avoid the battle. In that case one certainly might debouch by Wittenberg. But as the enemy still holds the initiative I shall only decide when I learn the situation tonight.

As regards the fate of Dresden, the Emperor hesitated for some time. On the afternoon of October 6, he sent for St. Cyr and instructed him to take command of the I and XIV Corps in order to defend it. About midnight, however, he sent for him again and told him he had changed his mind.

I shall fight a battle, without doubt. If I win I shall regret not having all my troops at hand. If I lose, then if I leave you here, you will have been of no use to me, and you will be hopelessly lost. After all, of what advantage is Dresden to me now? The place can no longer form the pivot of our operations, the district is too completely cleaned out to feed an Army .... Once the Elbe is frozen over it ceases to form an obstacle. I will choose another position; my right on Erfurt, centre along the Saale, the left on Magdeburg. It is a big, strong fortress which one can leave to itself as often as one chooses without fear that the enemy can carry it by a surprise assault.

Then, after dwelling in detail on the difficulties of fortifying Dresden, he continued:

Dresden is too near the mountains; as soon as I make the smallest movement from this town against the enemy's Army, it steps back again under their cover, as it has only a short way to go, and I have no means of cutting it off, as I cannot get behind it.

The result of this conversation was drafted into the form of an order, and next morning St. Cyr set about evacuating his advanced positions, not without severe fighting. Later in the day he received a counter-order from the Emperor, dated 10 a.m. (October 7), instructing him to remain in his position, as he had decided not to give up Dresden after all.

Probably no orders during the whole course of the campaign have evoked more criticism than the above. St. Cyr, in his *Memoirs,* has dealt with them at length, describing in detail the Emperor's manner on the several occasions, and it is indeed difficult to explain away the obvious vacillation they betray. But if one endeavours to focus the position from the Emperor's standpoint of certain victory, and remember the many plans seething in his mind as to his future conduct in that event, such as the occupation of Berlin, and the relief of the Oder garrisons; or a descent on the rear of the Bohemian Army should it venture forth into the Saxon plains, his motive becomes clearer. It is certain that the concentration of every available man, horse, and gun on the decisive point is a sound fundamental principle, but just as no engineer thinks of putting more metal into a bridge than is necessary to meet the maximum strain which experience shows can be brought to bear upon it, so a General, when obviously he has made sufficient provision for every emergency, is justified in employing the excess of his forces elsewhere. This is more especially the case since the actual striking power of an Army does not increase in direct proportion with its numbers, but may on the contrary lose by them, particularly where, as in this instance, the troops had to live on the district they traversed, and the roads were few and very indifferent.

As the Emperor only estimated the combined forces of the Silesian and Northern Armies at 100,000 men (a 20 per cent, under-estimate, as a matter of fact), he was surely justified in believing that with himself and 160,000 men he had made sufficient provision for all possible contingencies. Bernadotte, as we shall presently see, considered them more than ample.

Meanwhile, Blücher and Bernadotte after their passage across the Elbe, determined to march upon Leipzig, with a view to facilitating the exit of the Bohemian Army into the plains by diverting to themselves Napoleon's attention. In pursuance of this plan the Silesian Army was to reach the vicinity of Düben on October 8, and both Headquarters together were to enter Leipzig on the 9th. Following out these orders, Sacken reached Eilenburg, Langeron Düben, and Yorck Mühlbach. But the main body of the North Army, for some unexplained reason, remained halted at Jessnitz; and alarmed by a rumour of the approach of a French Corps from the direction of Magdeburg, Bernadotte sent back a strong force to guard his bridges at Rosslau. The whole Army was thus distributed over a depth of some forty miles, needing two whole days to close on its front for action. Notwithstanding the fact that they were operating in a friendly country, and possessed a great superiority in Cavalry, their knowledge of the French position was most vague. It was not until late in the afternoon, when the news reached them that the Emperor had left Dresden taking the road to Leipzig, whither a very large force had preceded him, that the full danger of the situation dawned upon the Allies. On the evening of October 8, 22 Infantry Divisions and 12 Cavalry Divisions, in all 150,000 men were closely concentrated under the Emperor himself, who was actually drafting the orders for the battle which he confidently expected to fight near Düben next morning.

During the previous days the Headquarters of the two Armies had discussed, on paper and verbally, the measures to be adopted in every emergency; and in the particular one that had now arisen, Blücher was to fall back on Wartenburg, whilst Bernadotte attacked the advancing French in flank. A proceeding which would, in fact, have resulted in the complete destruction of both Generals, for the Emperor in his *battalion carrée* formation was safe from anything which the North Army might attempt against him. But Blücher's obstinacy saved him from this pitfall. He was absolutely determined not to retreat, and his Staff knew it was impossible to move him; so using this knowledge as a fulcrum, they managed to open a door for escape.

In any event, the closest co-operation with Bernadotte was indispensable. Fortunately, it was common knowledge that Bernadotte had been most averse to the movement on Leipzig, and had strongly advocated the occupation of a defensive position behind the Saale.

Accordingly, an officer of the General Staff, Major Rühle von Lilienstein, was sent to Bernadotte by the Silesian Headquarters to give him the latest intelligence, and to suggest a recurrence to his previous plan of a position on the Saale. The Staff officer arrived late at night, and found the Crown Prince of Sweden in bed, but he was nevertheless immediately received, and duly made his report. Bernadotte having heard it, expressed his opinion that under the circumstances all the rules of War indicated an immediate retreat across the Elbe of both Armies, in order to cover Berlin. Von Rühle replied that the Silesian Headquarters attached no particular importance to Berlin. "The Russians had burnt Moscow, and they could sacrifice their capital also," further, that he knew for certain that Blücher would never consent to retreat, but would prefer to withdraw behind the Saale and thence extend a hand to the Bohemian Army. Asked by the Prince what authority he could show in support of his position, he replied that he had none, except his intimate personal knowledge of the character of his Chief.

Bernadotte appeared much struck with this assertion, and he then proposed himself that both Armies should revert to the original plan of the Saale position. It is suggested that in fact he believed Blücher would not dare to accept this responsibility. With this message then von Rühle returned to his Headquarters.

Needless to say Bernadotte, if he really entertained any such idea, was disappointed in the result. Blücher jumped at the offer, and forthwith the orders were drafted which enabled the Silesian Army to escape the blow which Napoleon had intended should fall upon it, by sacrificing all its communications and moving to its right, though not without some fighting and a series of most fortunate accidents.

Had the French Cavalry been at all equal to its duties, the direction of Blücher's march could hardly have escaped detection. But in fact the French Army lost touch of its adversary altogether, and Napoleon therefore had recourse to his favourite principle of marching against the most vital point in the enemy's possession, in order to compel him to turn round and fight in its defence.

In 1806 this had been the roads to Berlin, in 1813 it was again the roads to Berlin, but more particularly the bridges which the Allies had thrown over the Elbe; and throughout the 9th and 10th the French pursued this general direction; the Silesian Army continuing its movement to the Saale, and Bernadotte's marching to join them in a very half-hearted manner.

For October 11, the Emperor ordered Reynier (VII), Macdonald (XI), Bertrand (IV) and Sebastiani's Cavalry Corps to cross the river at Wittenberg, disperse the Prussian Corps of observation before that place, and move down the right bank of the river to capture and destroy all the bridges. This movement was to be supported by Souham's Corps (III) directed towards Dessau, and the Guards at Kemberg; all the Cavalry well to the front, and Marmont to remain behind in support at Düben, scouting towards Halle.

These orders, however, received very partial execution. The weather had again set in very wet, and the exhausted half-starved troops were quite incapable of reaching their assigned destinations, while the information they collected proved insufficient to establish with any certainty the whereabouts of their enemy's main body.

Napoleon therefore directed the movement to be continued on the following day, and for himself remained in Düben, impatiently awaiting further intelligence.

If we revert to the usual standpoint of criticism and imagine the Emperor as endeavouring to find a loophole of escape, his apparent hesitation at this point can easily be construed into anxiety and vacillation. The road for escape to Magdeburg down the right bank of the Elbe was absolutely open, and the enemy's parks, miles of which were seen by the advanced parties moving along the roads, guaranteed his subsistence, whilst Murat was free to retire at any moment either by Torgau or Wittenberg. Why then should he hesitate, or show any anxiety? But if we conceive him as bent on securing a really decisive success, it is quite clear that the strain upon his patience must have been immense, and sufficient to justify a certain shortness of temper. For now the idea was growing within him that a far bigger game than the mere destruction of the Northern and Silesian Armies was opening out for him.

These two Armies lay absolutely at his mercy. Tauentzien's force at Dessau had been driven over the Elbe in such disorder, that, in fact, it never rallied until it reached Berlin, ninety miles away, and a concentric advance of all his available forces must have placed Blücher and Bernadotte, wherever they stood, in an impossible position. But meanwhile to the southward, the Bohemian Army had at length left the shelter of the mountains for the plains and with every hour were laying themselves more and more open to his attack.

Instead of following boldly in the footsteps of the Emperor's forces, and taking Torgau and Würzen as their points of direction—in which case Napoleon might have found himself between two fires—they had moved to their left via Chemnitz and Altenberg, in order to avoid any risk of an offensive return on the part of the Emperor, and were nearing Naumburg on the Saale. Their right, on the night of the 12th, actually rested on Chemnitz, so that there was a great gap open to Napoleon's attack between that place and the mountains, and their direct communications with Bohemia were completely uncovered.[1]

Murat had hitherto easily held his opponents in check, and if Napoleon now joined him with his whole Army, he could count upon bringing 200,000 men on to the battlefield, a force which, under the Emperor's command, were more than sufficient to ensure success. Defeat of the Bohemian Army would almost certainly entail the break-up of the whole Alliance and a peace on terms of his own dictation. Under such conditions, the idea of safety for his own line of retreat must almost have seemed superfluous to Napoleon, yet since he still held Dresden, Meissen, Torgau and Wittenberg, with the resources of the Oder fortresses and Berlin behind him, his situation even in the event of defeat, could hardly have appeared desperate in his eyes, and one can easily understand both his impatience at the delay until all necessary information for the carrying out of his resolution was in his hands. At the same time the vein of optimism that runs through all his correspondence of the day is equally easy to understand.

The one doubt in his mind had been whether the Bohemian Army would give him battle, and when at length at 9.30 a.m. on October 12, a report from Murat arrived, stating that the Austrians were actually advancing towards Leipzig, and not towards Naumburg, as he had feared, his decision was instantly taken, and Berthier was instructed to prepare at once the necessary orders for a general counter-march of the whole French Army.

At 3.30 in the afternoon he wrote to Marmont a note which reveals his whole line of thought.

---

1. Actually the danger was not so grave as it appears. For some weeks negotiations had been in progress between Austria and Bavaria, and on October 8, the latter had agreed to join the Allies with all her forces; a retreat to the Danube through Bavaria was therefore always open to the Bohemian Army, but this was still unknown to Napoleon.

We have captured the enemy's bridges over the Elbe and it appears that Bernadotte's Army has retreated to the right bank. On the other side, the King of Naples is at Crobern in a position which I have ordered him to hold all the 13th. My intention is that whilst the King holds this position, you should march off at 3 a.m. tomorrow and take up a position on the Düben road with your left on Taucha. I am coming from Düben with the Old Guard to join you, and Curial's and Léfèbvre's Divisions are coming from Eilenburg, so that tomorrow about noon, we can unite 70,000 men about Leipzig. My whole Army will be concentrated on the 14th, and I shall give battle to the enemy with 200,000 men.

Later in the day again, a doubt appears to have crossed his mind whether Murat could hold his position throughout the 13th? But the only difference this makes in his disposition is to induce him to select a point of concentration on the Mulde nearer to his hand, at which to halt his troops if the necessity should arise, but a battle at all costs he is determined upon.

In the meantime the Silesian Army had taken up its position about Halle on the Saale, and the Northern Army lay some fifteen miles further down the stream between Wettin and Connern. The patrols of the Silesian Army had joined hands with those of the Bohemian Army and communication between the Headquarters was regularly established.

Deserters from the French Army, generally Saxons or Würtembergers, kept Blücher well informed of the French movements between Düben and Leipzig, but Bernadotte appears only to have received alarmist rumours from his bridges on the Elbe.

All through October 12, he had shown signs in his correspondence with Blücher of growing anxiety, and when at length the news of Ney's attack on Dessau reached him, he completely lost his head and ordered his own troops to concentrate forward on Cöthen; that is to say, if the reports on which he acted were well founded, he meant to commit the act of happy despatch, and at the same moment he wrote to Blücher to implore him to accompany him in this voluntary suicide.

Blücher, however, looked at the situation with far greater coolness. If Bernadotte's information was correct, it was clear that it was *too late* to retreat, and the greater the number of troops which Napoleon had massed on the north, the fewer there must necessarily be about Leipzig with Murat. The obvious plan, therefore, was to join the Bohemian Army in crushing the latter's forces. His (Blücher's) communications could look after themselves, for after all he had eaten up everything the country could contribute in the north whilst the south had almost escaped the ravages of recent War; and his guns and muskets took the same ammunition as the Austrians, Bavarians and French. Leipzig must fall into the hands of the Allies and was known to be well stocked with war material.

He therefore decided to continue his movement on Leipzig, and meanwhile set in motion every conceivable means of diplomatic pressure to induce the Crown Prince to renounce the idea of retreat and join him in his manoeuvre towards the Bohemian Army.

Whether the diplomatic pressure succeeded, or whether the greater fear of being left to face Napoleon single-handed prevailed, cannot now be decided, but in the night Bernadotte changed his mind and ordered his Army to follow and support Blücher. But the delay had left them so far behind that his troops arrived far too late to render assistance in the desperate combat of Möckern on the 16th.

As we have seen, on the night of October 12, the Bohemian Army lay with its right in Chemnitz and its left on Altenberg, but its advance, in spite of its extreme slowness (about six miles a day), had been so badly regulated, that portions of the troops were still far to the rear and a couple of days at least were needed to concentrate it for action.

For October 13, Schwarzenberg had instructed the leading units of his right wing to report to Wittgenstein in order to carry out a "forced" reconnaissance towards Leipzig. Owing to the usual delays in the circulation of orders, the troops did not reach their allotted positions of readiness till 4 p.m., when it was too late to carry out the proposed advance—a typical instance of the hopeless want of organization of the Staff service throughout the whole campaign, and the direct cause of the extraordinary slowness of all its operations. What prompted Schwarzenberg to this reconnaissance is not quite clear, for long before it could by any possibility have borne fruit, he issued orders for the whole Army to continue its movement to the left, towards Naumburg.

This order, however, evoked a storm of opposition, especially from the Prussians and Russians, and such pressure was brought to bear upon him that it was cancelled, and in its place fresh instructions were drawn up which pointed to an advance on Leipzig. And these rendered a battle inevitable.

As a preliminary Wittgenstein was directed to execute the postponed reconnaissance on the following morning (14th), and out of this developed the sharp action of Lisbertwolkwitz, notable for Murat's great Cavalry charges in masses; squadrons following one another at six horses' length distance; with which the more mobile Cavalry of the Allies, in spite of want of unity in the command, found no difficulty in dealing.[1]

Though the French Cavalry achieved nothing, their Infantry held their ground without difficulty, and thus Napoleon

1. Murat had at his disposal on this day the newly-formed 5th Cavalry Corps (Pajol), which included Milhaud's Division of Cuirassiers from Spain, the 4th Cavalry Corps (Kellermann), Berkheim's Division of the 1st Cavalry Corps and a Polish Cuirassier Regiment— in all 75 squadrons = 8,550 horses. Against these the Allies could only oppose 34 squadrons =4,000 horses until late in the afternoon, when another 15 squadrons, about 1,570 strong, appeared on the field. (Friedrichs iii, p. 454).

was led into taking up the position for the battle of the 16th, which, it has always seemed to me, was the primary cause of his failure, as the sequel will show.

The general result of the engagement was so far in favour of the Allies, that it became practically impossible for their Commander-in-Chief to avoid the battle, and the whole of the 15th was spent in reconnoitring the ground and preparing detailed orders for the attack. Relying on Langenau's local knowledge (as a Saxon officer he was reputed to be intimately acquainted with the ground) a first disposition was issued about noon, which had the extraordinary effect of breaking up the whole Allied Army into three commands; separated from one another by the unfordable streams of the Pleisse and Elster, which converge in the suburbs of Leipzig itself.

On the right a body of 72,000 men were to attack the position held by Murat resting its left on the Pleisse; in the centre 52,000 were to operate in the marshy and densely overgrown district between the Pleisse and the Elster, with the intention of turning Murat's left which lay in the village of Connewitz; and 19,000 under Gyulai were to attack the defile of Lindenau through which ran the main road from Leipzig to the west.

The defects of this disposition were so glaringly apparent that nearly the whole Russian Staff, including Barclay de Tolly, Diebitsch, Toll, and Jomini, approached Schwarzenberg to induce him to modify it. All their efforts, however, were in vain, and at length in despair they sought the Emperor Alexander and laid the matter before him; in no measured language it would seem, for Jomini went so far as to say that „one would imagine Napoleon must have dictated it in order to procure for himself the most decisive victory possible" (*Friedrichs,* vol. III, 11).

The Emperor Alexander, "surprised beyond measure at this unanimity between his Generals" *(ibid)* requested Schwarzenberg's attendance, and endeavoured to induce him to modify his plan. Even this was in vain, until at length the Emperor ended the interview by announcing his determination to dispose of all the Russian troops as he chose, which of course rendered an alteration of the plan inevitable. The Russo-Prussian Guards were withdrawn from the central command to Rotha, nearly ten miles from the probable battlefield, so that the possibility at least existed of bringing up the right wing during the course of the battle to 96,000 men, still far too few to encounter, with reasonable hope of success, 150,000 men under Napoleon in person.

The latter had hoped, as already pointed out, to have his troops in hand for an attack on this very day (18th) when under the circumstances success was, humanly speaking, assured; but, as already on several occasions during this campaign, he had over-estimated the marching powers of his men most materially. The weather had been bad, the roads almost bottomless seas of mud, and it had been impossible for the troops to reach their destinations in time. Nevertheless, bringing the Guards with him, the Emperor reached Leipzig about noon, and the cheers with which he was greeted carried the news of his arrival to the enemy's Headquarters, as once before at Dresden.

Viewed by the light of subsequent events, Schwarzenberg's conduct appears almost imbecile, yet, as we have seen, he had been selected by the almost unanimous consent of his contemporaries, indeed by the judgment of Napoleon himself, as a man of the greatest promise, and the only one possible under the circumstances for his position. Of his absolutely single-minded devotion to his duty the following letter, written by him to his wife after the stormy scenes of this day, is sufficient testimony:

> When I look out of my window at the almost innumerable camp fires spread out around me, when I reflect that opposed to me stands the greatest Leader of our

times, one of the greatest of all times indeed, then, my dearest, I must confess to you that my shoulders seem not strong enough to bear the load. But when I look up to the stars and remember that He who guides them in their courses has also pre-determined my career, if it is His will that the just cause, and I hold ours to be just, should conquer, then He will enlighten my conduct and give me strength. If He wills that we go under, my personal misfortune will only be the least of the sad consequences. If I survive defeat, I know I shall not on that account, my darling, seem of less account in your dear eyes. In either case, I have long since conquered my own ambition and egotism, and the judgment of the world will neither punish or reward me.[1]

This letter at least rings true, and only a great character in the best sense could have written it, and one hardly knows which to admire most, the character which could write it, or the wife to whom it was written. When such a man fails one must look far deeper into the chain of cause and effect to find the reason than it is possible to do here. Briefly, it may be said Napoleon controlled his times, Schwarzenberg was controlled by them; but the former only obtained his chance when the cohesion of society had been practically dissolved. How he would have fared under more stable surroundings such as those in which Schwarzenberg found himself entangled must remain an enigma for all time.

When the final Army order reached Wittgenstein, in chief command of the whole right wing, he proceeded to distribute his available force into five columns of unequal strength, in which all the existing commands were ignored. Russian Divisions and Prussian Brigades, even Regiments, were distributed about on no system at all; and though it was impossible for

---

1. Friedrichs quotes this from Theelen's *Erinnerungen aus dem Kriegsleben eines 82, jährigen Veteranen.*

his command to be concentrated within itself before noon, he ordered the leading detachments to commence the attack at 7 a.m., which meant a break up of their bivouacs long before daylight. Yet it seems quite possible that this typical piece of bad Staff management was really the most important factor in the day's success, for it took the French by surprise at a time when the Emperor had not yet completed his arrangements for the battle; and though nowadays it is impossible to trace in full detail the exact sequence of cause and effect, the best relations of the battle seem to reveal from the outset a want of co-ordination in its direction, unusual where Napoleon was present in person.

Prom the Emperor's instructions to Berthier, given out in the early morning of the 16th, it is clear that he meant to hold the direct attack of the Bohemian Army with Murat's command, *viz.*, the V, II, and VIII Corps, together with the 4th Cavalry Corps, on the line Connewitz-Liebertwolkwitz, whilst the IX and XI Corps with the 1st, 2nd, and 5th Cavalry Corps, pivoting on Liebertwolkwitz, swung in on the right of the Allies; and the Guards, VI and III Corps, and 3rd Cavalry Corps were to give the decision out of the centre, when "the battle was ripe." Altogether he had about 160,000 men, with 600 guns, against the 96,000 troops of the Allies, which as we have seen could only be engaged in succession, and not handled as a united whole.

But at the moment the attack began the XI Corps had not reached its position, and both the III and VI Corps found themselves held by the advance of the Prussians from the direction of Schlanditz, a possibility for which the Emperor had not made sufficient allowance.

However, the first rush of the Allies was easily repulsed; but, quite at variance with their usual custom, the repulsed troops refused to run away, and holding on to such cover as the ground afforded, they formed rallying points on which their reinforcements actually hastening to the roar of the guns formed in succession as they arrived. The accounts of this read exactly like those of the early battles of 1870; each detachment independently forcing its way to the front, with the superior Commanders in rear exerting no further influence on the troops engaged, except through such fresh troops as they could find to throw into the combat.

At length, about 11 a.m., Macdonald's Corps (XI) reached its preliminary position, initiated its turning movement, and about 2p.m., its attack having sufficiently developed, the Emperor ordered the whole line of Corps to advance; and Drouot with 84 guns galloped out to clear the way for Mortier and the Guards with case shot. But at this moment the unforeseen arrived. General Bordesoulle, with his Division of about 2,000 Cuirassiers in 18 Squadrons, suddenly decided to launch his whole force against a great Russian battery from whose fire the leading columns of the French Infantry were suffering severely. The attack was most gallantly ridden, and 26 guns had been put out of action, when from all sides the Cavalry of the Allies, by Brigades, Regiments, or even Squadrons, just as they came to hand, bore down upon the blown and disordered Squadrons of Bordesoulle's command. Then in turn, to rescue their comrades, all the remaining available Squadrons on the French side rode down into the *mêlée* which speedily formed.

The confusion which ensued has baffled all attempts at analysis; but, briefly, for about an hour and a half wild hordes of horsemen were hurled at one another, rallying and charging again and again and completely masking the fire of the guns on either side, and thus preventing their further advance. But when at last the turmoil ceased, the French opportunity was lost, the Russian and Prussian Guards had arrived on the scene, had occupied villages, woods and coppices, and against these fresh troops under cover, the French case fire could achieve nothing. Step by step the French fell back, and as darkness put an end to the fighting, they had been driven back to the limits of the position they had held in the morning.

The attack of the Austrians on the bridge at Connewitz had effected absolutely nothing, and thus it came to pass that at length Napoleon on a field of his own choice, with odds of nearly two to one in his favour, had been beaten by the sheer obstinate devotion to their cause of his individual enemies, and not at all by the skill of their leaders.

Thus failed one of the greatest, if not the greatest strategical conception in history; for had it succeeded Napoleon's success must have been final and irrevocable. Nothing the Silesian Army could have achieved on the other extremity of the battlefield could have altered the final result, and the Austrian centre columns between the Pleisse and Elster could not conceivably have extricated themselves from their hopeless predicament.

The cause of this incredible failure deserves more than a passing notice. In its simplest form it was merely this, the men of the Allied armies were wrought up to a white heat of patriotic enthusiasm, fanned by the spirit of revenge, and increased by the reaction throughout all the junior ranks against the *apparently* hopeless incompetence of their Commanders.[1] The French had fought for the honour of their arms and the personal devotion of their chiefs for their great Leader; but the hearts of the men in the ranks were not really in their work, for over-fatigue and privation had broken their spirits.

Still, the French Army, though it had failed, was not beaten, as the events of the next forty-eight hours were to prove.

The night which followed the battle of Leipzig was one of terrible suffering for both sides. The opposing forces lay

---

1. I stress the word "*apparently*" because in fact these men were not incompetent but were experienced veterans, each of whom knew more of battlefields than any living Europeans. They were simply the victims of their surroundings, as were ours too often in South Africa; but harassed men, longing to get at their enemy, never make allowances in these matters. This is the essential reason why troops should be taught from time to time in large masses and subjected to considerable marching privations. We cannot employ bullets in manoeuvres, but we can make things pretty miserable without them.

so close to one another that the utmost vigilance was necessary, and the actual fighting lines practically stood watch and watch all through the hours of darkness. There was no shelter for the wounded, who had to be left where they fell, and, though it rained all night, water except from the puddles in which men and horses had bled to death was hardly obtainable. Firewood, too, was so scarce that the men had to break up and burn saddle-trees, broken muskets and gun wheels, and the night was most bitterly cold. Exact statistics of the losses on this day are unattainable, but probably about 35,000 killed and wounded cumbered the ground on which the fighting had taken place, *i.e.*, a strip about four miles long by one wide, and around the villages (scenes of the fiercest fighting) the dead lay in swathes. Fortunately for those who had been wounded at first, no quarter was either asked or given, thus several thousands escaped the most awful suffering, prolonged, in some cases, for more than a week before they could be moved or help be brought to them.

Napoleon had his tent pitched in the midst of his Guards' bivouac, and here he spent a wakeful night, while messenger after messenger brought him tidings containing nothing but evil.

Worst of all there was the news of Marmont's defeat at Möckem—about four miles north east of Leipzig. Marmont, on the 14th, had been sent from Taucha by Napoleon with a general mission, to keep the Silesian Army at bay, whilst Ney's command filed into the town behind him. Ney to support him, if necessary, as it was of vital importance to ensure the arrival of all the ammunition trains. On the morning of the 16th, the V Corps had safely passed, the III Corps was in the act of passing, and the VII was due during the early hours of the afternoon. Napoleon had summoned both the VI and III Corps to the main battlefield, believing that distance alone would prevent the Silesian Army from reaching the scene of action in time to take effective part in it. Both Corps were actually moving in accordance with this order, when such heavy masses of the enemy appeared in sight that Marmont decided to halt and face them, while Ney promised him the assistance of the III Corps. Marmont deployed his men across a low elevation of the ground, his left resting on Möckern and his right on Klein Widderitzsch. Here he was assailed by Yorck's Corps and part of Sacken's, whilst Langeron's followed in echelon on their left rear.

The combat which ensued was most obstinate and sanguinary. Möckern was taken and retaken over and over again, and time after time the Prussians threw themselves upon the French lines. At length came the psychological moment. Marmont was moving his last reserves into the line, when out of a cloud of powder smoke a great mass of Prussian Cavalry suddenly charged down upon their flank. Panic ensued and spread along the position, which, attacked again by the Prussian Infantry, was carried all along the line.

Marmont left some 6,000 to 7,000 men on the ground, and Yorck's Infantry was reduced from 16,120 according to the morning states of the 16th, to 9,000 at nightfall. Langeron lost 1,500 men; Sacken's troops only reached the field at the last moment, and suffered less than did the others. It was in this combat in particular that the Prussian *Landwehr* won its enduring fame. Hitherto they had given the old officers, accustomed to the faultless march discipline which the regular troops had inherited from the old Frederickian Army, reason to complain bitterly of their conduct, and this unsteadiness seems to have inspired mistrust of their fighting spirit. Hence they had rarely been given a chance of showing what they could do when occasion demanded a supreme effort. On this day, however, they exceeded all possible expectations; and the example they afforded is at present being freely cited by German Socialists as an argument for still further reduction in the time of service in the existing Army, and is being so bitterly resented by the Regular Army, that even Major Friedrichs is hardly fair to them in consequence.

Marmont's defeat certainly aggravated the dangers of Napoleon's situation, and possibly had he been aware that a fresh Corps of Russians under Benningsen, 30,000 strong, was in full march upon the Dresden-Leipzig road to close the gap between the Parthe and the right wing of the Allies, he might even then have reconsidered his position and determined to break back to the northward on Wittenberg and Dessau, by the Same roads by which he and Ney had just arrived.

If Blücher and Bernadotte endeavoured to interpose, his combined force could practically march out over their bodies, for with nearly two to one odds in his favour, victory must still have seemed almost a foregone conclusion. Moreover, there was always the very strong probability that Blücher and Bernadotte would never venture on such a bold stroke, but would manoeuvre to their right to join Gyulai in front of Lindenau. Napoleon naturally believed this General to be still in the position he had occupied during the day, he could not know that Gyulai had been ordered to move across to his right to join the Main Army, leaving the great road to the Rhine practically open for the French retreat. As far as the Emperor's knowledge extended, there was still ample time to crush the Bohemian Army first of all, and his line of retreat could not be seriously compromised for another forty-eight hours at least. It was probably this line of reasoning which led Napoleon to decide to renew the battle on the 18th. Meanwhile, probably to create divided counsel at the Allied Headquarters, he endeavoured to reopen diplomatic relations by a proposal to treat for peace, with the view of putting a stop to further useless effusion of blood, for nobody could be more humane than Napoleon when it suited his purpose.

The Allies, however, were in no humour to treat, and with full knowledge of the near approach of Benningsen, they closed their whole Army in on its right (thereby uncovering the road to the Rhine, as already mentioned), and arranged with the Commanders of the North and Silesian Armies that these two forces should march off by their left, cross the Parthe, some five miles above Leipzig, and join hands with Benningsen, when the semicircle around the French would be completed, its outer flanks resting on the Elster and Parthe respectively, both being susceptible of easy defence.

During the day, Blücher also attacked the north-west suburb of Leipzig (through which run the roads to Halle and Düben) in order to conceal still further his ultimate intentions.

Napoleon, on his part, formed up his Army in a semicircle, his left still on the Pleisse about Connewitz, his centre at Probst Heyda, and his left thrown back towards the Parthe, whose marshy banks appeared impracticable for troops attacking from the north. Very strong outposts still held the ridge on which the fighting of the previous day had taken place, thus the dispositions of the French Army were entirely concealed, and the main position had this further advantage, that the Allies in advancing to the attack had, of necessity, to disclose their masses to sight, and found no sheltering woods or copses to conceal them as on the 16th.

Ney held the command of the whole of the whole of the right wing, Murat of the left; Napoleon himself with his Guards and Cavalry covered the junction at the centre, and could move unimpeded to either flank as occasion required. Only Bertrand (IV Corps) and the garrison of Leipzig were absent from the battlefield, the former remaining to cover the exit of the defile of Lindenau.

The exact strength of the French Army cannot now be ascertained. Probably 160,000 men with about 650 guns stood in the ranks on the morning of the 18th, and against this force the Allied Sovereigns disposed of no fewer than 295,000 men with 1,500 guns, of which some 100,000 never came into action at all.

It is impossible nowadays to trace in detail the vicissitudes of the struggle which followed. The French left and centre held their ground until the evening, and the decision was given by the junction of the Silesian and Northern Armies with Benningsen's column, which took place about 2 p.m.[1]

But Napoleon had already realized that further resistance was useless; his first orders initiating a retreat by Lindenau had gone out at 11 a.m., and now fighting was only continued to gain space for withdrawal.

He himself spent the night on the battlefield, snatching a few minutes' sleep sitting upright on a peasant's chair by the bivouac fire, surrounded by his Staff. About 5 a.m. a chance round shot struck the embers of the fire, scattering the crowd. The Emperor woke up, and continued at once dictating the necessary orders.

About 10 a.m. he rode through the town, and took the road to the Rhine, moving through all the turmoil with the same stern set face which his men had learnt to know in the Russian retreat just a year before.

Eventually the Allies carried Leipzig by storm, and owing to the premature destruction of the bridges a large number of French prisoners fell into their hands; but of a pursuit in the real sense of the word there was no indication, and in a few days the Emperor again had in his hands a total force exceeding 80,000 combatants, with which he completely routed the attempt made by a combined force of Austrians and Bavarians (about 50,000 strong, under Wrede) to intercept his retreat at Hanau.

Here we must leave him, whilst we try briefly to formulate the lesson of this most extraordinary, and *strategically most successful* of his campaigns, for strategically his concentration at Leipzig will ever remain his masterpiece. In his early campaigns he was handling little more than an Army Corps; in 1814 again his actual effectives mustered little more, and in

---

1. About 2 p.m. also some 3,000 Saxons went over to the Allies from the French left. Much has been made of this incident in popular histories, but in fact, it was quite insignificant, and exercised no influence whatever on the course of the battle.

both he was leading troops animated almost with fanaticism. But in this great struggle in the heart of an enemy's country, miles away from his ultimate base, he controlled Armies, he imparted to them his own spirit, and managed even to make good the mistakes of his Generals. But the fighting which centred around Dresden marked the limit of his powers, and it is interesting to note the essential reason why it was so. If we compare the conditions with which he had to contend from the Armistice to the end of September, we find the same enemies, the same masses of men, and the same subordinate Commanders, only whereas the enemy had become bolder, Napoleon's men and officers had grown more and more war weary, the latter indeed were often despondent, yet whereas in the earlier part of the campaign his conduct is marked by painful indecision (never due, by the way, to ignorance of his enemies' positions, but to inability to control their intentions) in the latter, once he had definitely decided to hold on to Dresden, we find him acting always with the fixed determination to inflict upon his opponents the maximum amount of punishment possible. As I have pointed out above, critics hitherto, judging him by the final result, have insisted on regarding him as a hunted animal seeking a loophole of escape, whereas in fact his anxiety for the future, in so far as any genuine feeling of the kind can be proved to exist (see Friedrichs' comments on Yorck von Wartenberg's account of events at Düben) *was always as to the magnitude of the result to be achieved, and not its achievement, that, he believed to be beyond question secured to his side.* The only one essential difference between these two phases of the war lies in the fact that about Dresden, force of circumstances compelled him to adopt the defensive, whereas in the end he was free to act as assailant, and the measure of the advantage which the latter form enjoys over the former can be measured by the startling resuscitation of all his powers, once Blücher's march to join Bernadotte enabled him to change his rôle from defender to that of aggressor.

It is clear that throughout the Dresden episode, from the moment indeed that his memory failed him in the middle of his letter to Vandamne on August 23, he was no longer able to control events, and the evidence available for every day shows the gradual breakdown of his powers. The most elastic mind in the world, however, can scarcely throw off the effects of such severe overstrain in forty-eight hours; and his men and officers could hardly thus easily shake off the depressing influences of hunger, useless exertion, and impending retreat. Yet once he was at liberty to act as he chose and to dictate situations, he mastered the whole situation easily, and if, as alleged, he appeared worried and impatient for news when at Düben, well! any man who has ever been compelled to face great odds and to play for really high stakes can understand his frame of mind.

A further point brought out by this campaign is the purely *relative* value attaching to communications. Theoretically Napoleon's line was severed again and again by organized raids made in considerable force, but he never for one moment allowed these interruptions to hinder his designs. Both Blucher's and Bernadotte's communications lay open for nearly a month, and those of the Bohemian Army for about a fortnight, yet the Emperor simply disdained to strike at either, preferring to direct his blows at the Field Armies themselves. The curious thing to note is, *that no decision became possible until practically all parties had renounced the usual rules of the game,* and then at last it fell to the side which, according to all precedent, had placed itself in the most unfavourable position conceivable. This brings us to the root of the whole matter, and shows beyond possibility of discussion wherein the Art of the Leader really lies, *viz.*, in the correct appreciation of the relative fighting power of the opposing forces. Napoleon lost the campaign of 1813, *not because his communications were cut* (they were not), *but because he underrated the determination of the soldiers and subordinate of-*

ficers who opposed him. But when we recall how. often he had driven the long service veteran soldiers of all three nations before him, this mistake is seen to be natural; and for that very reason it brings out more clearly *the necessity of studying the very soul of a Nation, and realizing the difference that a really burning patriotism can make in the efficiency of its Army.*

According to any peace time standard of efficiency that can be conceived, these Prussian, Austrian and Russian levies must have appeared to their Generals of the old school as the veriest rabble; many of the former carried only extemporized pikes, and amongst the latter even bows and arrows were still to be found, and discipline in the old sense was so far to seek that men left the colours casually for a week or two, returning after a pleasant rest with their friends, quite ignorant of the fact that they had rendered themselves liable to the death penalty, which, of course, it was impossible to enforce.

Away from the enemy, their conduct was sometimes disgraceful. Tauentzien's men in the retreat to Berlin, about October 12, broke loose from all restraint, and plundered the villages and suburbs of their own people like the veriest *banditti.* But then, we must remember that they were more than half-starved and equally insufficiently clad. Even in the Silesian Army, before Bautzen, deserters from Prussian Cavalry Regiments formed themselves into regular gangs of marauders, waylaying and plundering in the wake of their Army, whereas in the retreat from Jena, the old Prussian soldiers did not even dare to break up a rail fence for necessary firewood without permission. Yet., in spite of all these departures from the narrow path, and notwithstanding the fact that more than nine-tenths of the whole were conscripts (and none too willing ones either) these Armies, as a whole, endured an almost unexampled strain. It was, of course, impossible in the space at my disposal, to enter into the daily encounters in any detail, but the fact remains that throughout the whole, month of September, both the Bohemian and Silesian Armies were fighting more or less on every day. Sometimes in retreat, sometimes in advance, and in encounters *far exceeding in severity* the so-called "disasters" of the Boer War. And all this in the midst of privations and horrors of which the present generation has very little or no idea. It was the fighting backwards and forwards over the same ground, and bivouacking night after night among the unburied dead and uncared for wounded that was so frightful a strain on the courage of the troops, especially the younger men. Things were bad also in the French Army, but in Napoleon's presence men fought with the certainty of victory, and with such blind confidence in his leadership that a retreat seemed only a stepping stone to fresh success; but in the Bohemian Army there was absolutely no confidence in the leading, and from the Corps Commanders downwards men felt they were being uselessly sacrificed.

Yet in face of the enemy these same men fought till sixty per cent, of casualties in a battalion became quite a common standard of loss, in spite of which the survivors were ready to fall in and fight again the next morning! Undoubtedly it was this determination which finally led to their national deliverance, and this standard would, I submit, *have been sooner attained, had the level of general intelligence and patriotism been sufficiently high to have brought the whole of the troops to the colours without compulsion.*

It must be remembered that very few indeed of these men had the slightest love of fighting for its own sake and that most were thrown into the full sweep of the War with only the most rudimentary training. No doubt they regretted their deficiencies in this respect after very little experience, but the point is, that in spite of them they succeeded where better trained men had very often failed. Now the lesson for us in all this campaign is the necessity of concentrating more on the spirit of our Army than on its externals.

Again, I must not be understood as wanting to underrate the importance of drill and regularity in administration—on the contrary I have always stood out for the utmost attainable steadiness and precision of drill, and have been roundly abused in consequence—but I do most earnestly deprecate the present attitude of mind which insists on condemning as absolutely without fighting value our Auxiliary Forces, because they fall short of a purely conventional peace time standard of organization and training. Admittedly, these defects will have to be paid for in blood and in much additional anxiety to the commanders, but the fact will always remain that, with a determined man at their head, troops willing to die for their country can still be led to victory. It is not by the skill which troops have acquired in dodging losses on the training ground, *but by the amount they are ready to bear, that the fate of Nations is decided.*

LEONAUR

ALSO FROM LEONAUR
AVAILABLE IN SOFTCOVER OR HARDCOVER WITH DUST JACKET

SEPOYS, SIEGE & STORM *by Charles John Griffiths*—The Experiences of a young officer of H.M.'s 61st Regiment at Ferozepore, Delhi ridge and at the fall of Delhi during the Indian mutiny 1857.

CAMPAIGNING IN ZULULAND *by W. E. Montague*—Experiences on campaign during the Zulu war of 1879 with the 94th Regiment.

THE STORY OF THE GUIDES *by G. J. Younghusband*—The Exploits of the Soldiers of the famous Indian Army Regiment from the northwest frontier 1847 - 1900..

ZULU: 1879 *by D.C.F. Moodie & the Leonaur Editors*—The Anglo-Zulu War of 1879 from contemporary sources: First Hand Accounts, Interviews, Dispatches, Official Documents & Newspaper Reports.

THE RECOLLECTIONS OF SKINNER OF SKINNER'S HORSE *by James Skinner*—James Skinner and his 'Yellow Boys' Irregular cavalry in the wars of India between the British, Mahratta, Rajput, Mogul, Sikh & Pindarree Forces.

TOMMY ATKINS' WAR STORIES 14 FIRST HAND ACCOUNTS—Fourteen first hand accounts from the ranks of the British Army during Queen Victoria's Empire Original & True Battle Stories Recollections of the Indian Mutiny With the 49th in the Crimea With the Guards in Egypt The Charge of the Six Hundred With Wolseley in Ashanti Alma, Inkermann and Magdala With the Gunners at Tel-el-Kebir Russian Guns and Indian Rebels Rough Work in the Crimea In the Maori Rising Facing the Zulus From Sebastopol to Lucknow Sent to Save Gordon On the March to Chitral Tommy by Rudyard Kipling

CHASSEUR OF 1914 *by Marcel Dupont*—Experiences of the twilight of the French Light Cavalry by a young officer during the early battles of the great war in Europe.

TROOP HORSE & TRENCH *by R. A. Lloyd*—The experiences of a British Lifeguardsman of the household cavalry fighting on the western front during the First World War 1914-18.

THE EAST AFRICAN MOUNTED RIFLES *by C. J. Wilson*—Experiences of the campaign in the East African bush during the First World War.

THE FIGHTING CAMELIERS *by Frank Reid*—The exploits of the Imperial Camel Corps in the desert and Palestine campaigns of the First World War.

Lightning Source UK Ltd.
Milton Keynes UK
06 April 2010

152353UK00001B/247/A